PRAISE FOR *NOTHIN*

"In this beautifully written memoir, Marlena Fiol tells a painful though ultimately inspirational story of difficulty and redemption. In her account of being raised in a sometimes-abusive Mennonite family in rural Paraguay, she shows how the path to family reconciliation can come through compassion and acceptance of others, rather than through insistence on their change. She also illustrates the important ways that connections to family—even to those who have been hurtful—can sometimes provide the greatest sources of strength and meaning."
— Joshua Coleman, PhD, author of *When Parents Hurt: Compassionate Strategies When You and Your Grown Child Don't Get Along*

"Novelist Ernest Hemingway said, 'The world breaks everyone and afterward many are strong at the broken places.' Some of the broken individuals emerge not just strong, but triumphant. That's Marlena Fiol's journey in *Nothing Bad Between Us: A Mennonite Missionary's Daughter Finds Healing in Her Brokenness.* I found enormous inspiration and encouragement in this beautifully written account. This book could have been written only by someone possessed of uncommon love, compassion, and empathy. For anyone who has been broken and is in need of healing, please put *Nothing Bad Between Us* at the top of your list."
— Larry Dossey, MD, *New York Times* bestselling author of *One Mind: How Our Individual Mind Is Part of a Greater Consciousness and Why It Matters*

"I found Marlena's story riveting and spellbinding. *Nothing Bad Between Us* is a true story of healing, deep reflection, raw emotion, and triumph. Marlena has been able to see through her own pain in order to encourage and help bring healing to others. Highly recommended."
— Misty Griffin, author of *Tears of the Silenced: An Amish True Crime Memoir of Childhood Sexual Abuse, Brutal Betrayal, and Ultimate Survival*

"This is one of the most moving and, ultimately, hopeful books I have ever read. We think we know our academic friends and colleagues. We meet them as adults and learn about their families. Perhaps we hear about their childhoods. But we don't appreciate the complexity of what has made them the people they are, the interweaving of suffering and joy that composes their lives. Marlena Fiol's profound and courageous book is a significant gift to all of us in sharing these sufferings and joys. It is, in many ways, a story of forgiveness and redemption, for others and oneself, as these unfold over a lifetime."

—Jean M. Bartunek, PhD, Robert A. and Evelyn J. Ferris chair, professor of management and organization at Boston College and former president of the Academy of Management

"Marlena Fiol's story rings so true to me, starting with the characteristics and history we share: Mennonite childhoods, academic careers, mothers of two children, daughters of strong fathers, and memoirists. I was never beaten by my father nor shamed by the church the way Fiol was. Nor did I grow up in a multilingual household with a recent history of religious persecution. However, we as readers love stories not because they are so much like our own but because they contain universal truths in concrete form. If they are especially deep and powerful stories, they bloom like native plants in the home soil. This book finally arrives in the place where it began, reaching a hard-won level of forgiveness that not only will move readers but cause them to search their own souls, looking for the place where they too can locate the love and peace they have craved all their lives."

—Shirley H. Showalter, PhD, former professor and president, Goshen College; former foundation executive, The Fetzer Institute; and author of *Blush: A Mennonite Girl Meets a Glittering World*

"For all of us on the journey of life and love, Marlena Fiol reminds us that the bonds between us and our parents are perhaps life's strongest. And may require the most work. And a large dose of forgiveness. At times poignant and pained, *Nothing Bad Between Us* reminds us, as the author says, how important it is to 'feel the salve of compassionate memory.' "

—Doug Bradley, author of *Who'll Stop the Rain: Respect, Remembrance, and Reconciliation in Post-Vietnam America* and coauthor of *We Gotta Get Out of This Place: The Soundtrack of the Vietnam War*

"With unflinching honesty, Marlena Fiol traces her journey from a rebellious childhood, rejected by both her Mennonite church and her devout father, to healing and reconciliation. As a physician and worldwide tai chi teacher, I find it especially remarkable that the healing did not arise out of finding logical points of agreement. Instead, it was grounded in one of the most fundamental principles of tai chi, that through receiving and redirecting the energy beneath harmful words and actions, it is possible to neutralize conflicts and move toward peaceful resolution. I highly recommend this book for anyone wishing to end negative cycles of reactivity in a relationship."

—Paul Lam, MD, founder of the Tai Chi for Health Institute, and author of *Born Strong: From Surviving the Great Famine to Teaching Tai Chi to Millions*

"Dreams, principles, and values deeply inform our personal narratives, the stories of our life that shapes how we live. Marlena Fiol's fearless recollection of life with her father reminds us that no matter how complete and noble the narrative, we need to remember to say *Thank you, What do you think?, I'm sorry*, and *I love you*. If not, even the noblest narrative will cast an overbearing shadow on others, especially our children. Thankfully, Marlena's sometimes self-destructive struggle with her father's shadow ends in recovery and reconciliation. In time, she was able to author her own life. And yes, even her father came to see that life was better when he freed those he loved to be themselves. This is a sometimes tough but always inspiring read."

—Jim Walsh, PhD, Arthur F. Thurnau professor at the University of Michigan and former president of the Academy of Management

"Of the infinite ways to tell a life story, Marlena has found words to take us deeply into her experience through the lens of her relationship with our broken, amazing, and beloved father. She does so with courage and vulnerability. Though I find it impossible to read this story with any kind of objectivity, I am a witness to the pain and the healing that they both experienced as they struggled to find what all our hearts so deeply long for, that safe haven in one another."

—Mary Lou Bonham, the sister of Marlena Fiol, marriage and family therapist, and licensed professional counselor

"In this powerful memoir, Marlena Fiol stays grounded in the reality of life and the imperfect people who are all just doing the best they can. Human love is complicated because it is merely human: not all that wise, not all that enduring, not all that pure. And so it is that we are saved by forgiveness and compassion for self as well as for others. Thus, there is a resurrection in this narrative, and that is where we can be hopeful. In this book, we come in the end to a quiet peace, joy, and even a divine love that moves and heals despite human brokenness."

—Stephen G. Post, PhD, director of the Center for Medical Humanities, Compassionate Care and Bioethics; professor of Family, Population and Preventive Medicine, Stony Brook University; and bestselling author of *God and Love on Route 80: The Hidden Mystery of Human Connectedness*

"Reconciliation can't happen unless people commit to entering the brokenness and pain to seek a new way forward. It requires perseverance, honesty, and humility. It is not easy. But on the other side, a restored relationship emerges— not the same as before, but beautiful and special. In *Nothing Bad Between Us*, Marlena Fiol bravely describes the process of reconciliation with her father. The pain and brokenness are evident, but so too is grace. Her story will inform others that risking reconciliation can bring new beauty to their families, churches and communities."

—Alan Claassen Thrush, Mennonite Central Committee

"Marlena's story is a modern odyssey: a life's journey punctuated with significant obstacles—some imposed and some self-inflicted, but all tests in finding a way to her personal and spiritual home. These are life-defining tests: public humiliation and exclusion from the faith of her missionary family, a life-threatening medical condition that left her with virtually no chance of creating the family she viewed as life-fulfilling, and her most enduring personal test—the humiliation of being physically abused and publicly disowned by her beloved but stern and uncompromising father. She passes all these tests with storied victories. She is triumphant in her life-odyssey, not by intervention from the gods, but by a more relatable, mortal means—a life well lived."

—Robert J. Meeker, EdD, president of SOI Systems Inc. and developer of Educational Systems

"Promise. Failure. Redemption. Forgiveness. Love. Marlena takes us to very dark places—places that most people fear to go, even in the sheltered security of their own minds. The rawness of her revelations makes us ache for her, hoping that she will find her way out of the darkness and pain. Triumphantly, she discovers the power of love and forgiveness. This is not a 'love conquers all' story, but rather a story of dogged persistence through her refusal to let herself be defined by others' perceptions. In the end, she preserves the fierce autonomy she displayed as a child but tempers it as an adult with an awareness of human fallibility. We may want to be good, but goodness often lies beyond our grasp. It's ok to settle for 'nothing bad.' "

—Howard E. Aldrich, PhD, Kenan Professor of Sociology, University of North Carolina at Chapel Hill

"Otherness comes in a variety of forms and legacies. Marlena Fiol's account of growing up a German American girl raised by Mennonite missionary parents in a leper colony in Paraguay poignantly captures the familial struggles and existential angst of growing up 'Other.' In a time of unprecedented migration and mobility, her journey of alienation, self-awareness, and ultimate self-healing offers hope and guidance for all who fall outside the mainstream."

—Mary Yoko Brannen, MBA, PhD, Dr. Merc. H.C. Honorary professor of International Business, Copenhagen Business School, Professor Emerita, San Jose State University

"It's rare to read a book with such intimate and personal details of a rebellious young woman growing up and maturing into motherhood. When it is set against the backdrop of a Mennonite community in Paraguay and her strained relationship with her father, a respected elder, it is especially daring. Memorable!"

—Kerry Cannon, bronze sculptor, creator of Ceramic Break Sculpture Park, Australia

"Marlena Fiol poignantly explores the multiplicity of relationships as they unfolded through various stages in her life...father-daughter, girl-boy, seeker-religion, lover-beloved, wife-husband, and mother-children. As we witness in her telling, strength, courage, vulnerability, and forgiveness allow the healing movement from judgment to compassion in wounded relationships. Her work is an important reminder to me about how dynamic and ever-changing relationships can be, and yet how crucial to my own pilgrimage."

—Daniel Martin, cofounder and president of Pension Planners Northwest, a retirement plan consulting firm

"*Nothing Bad Between Us* is a courageous story of both bringing to light family/community secrets and forgiving those who have been emotionally unavailable to us, failed to protect us, or even abused us. Marlena shows us that the path to surviving these kinds of abuses and neglect, while not linear, is achievable. It is through the truth, no matter how painful for all, that we can build a better future for ourselves, those we love, and the larger community."

—Dawn Tankersley, EdD, early childhood specialist

"Dr. Marlena Fiol shares her personal story of navigating her life journey to embrace authentic love, forgiveness, and healing in her latest book, *Nothing Bad Between Us*. But it is not just her story, for her book touches on everyone's longing to understand and experience authentic love. Much in the way that Joseph Campbell's *Hero's Story* is everyone's story, Dr. Fiol helps each reader feel the touch points to their own journey toward forgiveness and healing."

—Steven Gurgevich, PhD, licensed psychologist specializing in psychotherapy and hypnotherapy

"*Nothing Bad Between Us* is the compelling and deeply moving story of Marlena Fiol's journey to her authentic self. Raised in Paraguay, where her Mennonite parents founded a leprosy colony, Marlena struggled against the strictures and expectations of the church and her father's often brutal ways of trying to control his rebellious child. And as happens with a childhood where expectations overpower the true self, the struggle continues into adulthood, even when the parents are far away. Marlena Fiol is a fierce searcher with a willingness to examine herself and her own frailties and find compassion in others through this. With a pure and honest voice, Marlena invites you on the complicated journey of love."

—Jackie Shannon Hollis, author of *This Particular Happiness: A Childless Love Story*

"My dog hated Marlena Fiol's *Nothing Bad Between Us: A Mennonite Missionary's Daughter Finds Healing in Her Brokenness*. She is usually quite tolerant of my reading choices because she knows she can easily distract me and I will put down my reading to tend to her every whim. Once I began *Nothing Bad Between Us*, however, I was a goner. I simply had to finish the story of Marlena's childhood: in Paraguay, in a leper colony, with a brilliant and brutal father amidst a judgmental community of Mennonite missionaries. How many ways could this go wrong for a girl-child who was perhaps more brilliant and stubborn than her pious father? Marlena's story is one of spiritual struggle wrapped in adventure."

—Karen Brazeau, former director of Oregon's Juvenile Justice System and associate director of the Oregon Department of Education.

"*Nothing Bad Between Us* by Marlena Fiol is a deeply personal reflection on an evolving life. It is a story in three parts—the one she suffered as a child, the one she escaped to, and the one she chose. Fiol reflects on events and their meaning in intimate detail, especially the complicated relationship with her heroic and sometimes-abusive father. Anyone struggling with the complexities of relationships with significant others will benefit from reading this book. It is everyone's story at some level, but a story that only a few can sort out and resolve in a way that leads to joy for having had those experiences."

—Larry Peters, PhD, Emeritus faculty at The Neeley School of Business, TCU, and author of *The Simple Truths About Leadership*

"Revolving around the relationship between daughter and father, *Nothing Bad Between Us* is at once a brave, vulnerable, unflinching, warm, disturbing, tragic, and ultimately inspirational story that deftly dismantles our often-simplistic cultural accounts about what love is and what it 'should' be. If you've ever struggled to live up to your own and others' often unrealistic expectations of what it means to be a loving child, friend, coworker, parent, partner, or other role in an important relationship, this book can help you find the insights and strength to accept and forgive yourself and those you are trying to love. If you can do that, you are not promised a perfect relationship, but one where you can honestly say, 'Doa ess nuscht tweschen ons.' ('There's nothing bad between us.')"

—Michael G. Pratt, PhD, O'Connor Family professor, director of the PhD program in Management & Organization Department at Boston College

"In *Nothing Bad Between Us*, Marlena takes readers to her secret safe place in the forest, through intimate heartbreak and the love and pain of one family's journey, ending with hard-earned forgiveness and reconciliation. The work she has done to evolve physically, emotionally, cognitively, and spiritually will inspire you to face difficult challenges in your own life with courage and vulnerability."

—Rita Berglund, psychotherapist, retreat leader, and author of *An Alphabet about Kids with Cancer*

"Marlena Fiol, PhD, has masterfully blended her professional expertise in identity and learning with her own raw identity-changing experiences to bring us this vulnerable and inspirational story of personal transformation. Honest and brave in its detail, *Nothing Bad Between Us* begins as a heartrending account of a young girl escaping the confines of her strict and often abusive Mennonite community in Paraguay and ultimately offers a stirring testament to the power of authenticity and forgiveness."

> —Elaine Romanelli, PhD, Emeritus Faculty and senior associate dean, McDonough School of Business, Georgetown University

"Marlena Fiol offers us inroads to our own reflection, redemption, and growth by describing her incredible story in *Nothing Bad Between Us: A Mennonite Missionary's Daughter Finds Healing in Her Brokenness*. Fiol grew up in a Low-German Mennonite community in Paraguay. Her missionary parents were known as experts in the treatment of leprosy. This backdrop adds an additional layer of richness to what would be a powerful story in any setting. From my perspective, with a focus on innovation and change, I learned new ways of seeing the behavior and beliefs of others and then being able to create new approaches built on those foundations. This is a personal and powerful story, and I find myself returning to its ideas often when struggling to blend my perspective with others."

> —Terri Griffith, Keith Beedie Chaired professor of Innovation and Entrepreneurship, Simon Fraser University, and author of *The Plugged-In Manager: Get in Tune with Your People, Technology, and Organization to Thrive*

"In deeply personal stories, Marlena Fiol explores the opposing pulls of belonging and identity, approval and authority. Family vignettes spanning a lifetime peel away layers of complexity as father and daughter negotiate absolute belief and fragile reality. Yet brutal judgment gives way to deep love as the author finds resolution of these same internal contradictions just in time for—and perhaps through—full reconciliation. A thoroughly engaging and spiritually challenging read!"

> —Tom Bellamy, PhD, professor emeritus of education, University of Washington Bothell

NOTHING
BAD
BETWEEN US

NOTHING
BAD
BETWEEN US

A MENNONITE MISSIONARY'S
DAUGHTER FINDS HEALING
IN HER BROKENNESS

Marlena Fiol, PhD

CORAL GABLES

Published by Mango Publishing Group, a division of Mango Media Inc.

Cover Design, Layout & Design: Morgane Leoni
Cover Photography: © Anneka / Shutterstock
Tree Illustration: © galunga.art / Adobe Stock
Author Photo: © Chad Thompson at Monkey C Media

For permission requests, please contact the publisher at:
Mango Publishing Group
2850 S Douglas Road, 2nd Floor
Coral Gables, FL 33134 USA
info@mango.bz

For special orders, quantity sales, course adoptions and corporate sales, please email the publisher at sales@mango.bz. For trade and wholesale sales, please contact Ingram Publisher Services at customer.service@ingramcontent.com or +1.800.509.4887.

Nothing Bad Between Us: A Mennonite Missionary's Daughter Finds Healing in Her Brokenness

Library of Congress Cataloging-in-Publication number: 2020940937
ISBN: (print) 978-1-64250-358-6, (ebook) 978-1-64250-359-3
BISAC Category Code BIO022000, BIOGRAPHY & AUTOBIOGRAPHY / Women

Printed in the United States of America

Disclaimer: The author has related the events in this book as factually as possible, based on her memory, written documents, and conversations with others. In a few instances, she has changed names and identifying characteristics to protect the privacy of others without changing the facts relevant to the story.

This book is for you, Dad.
You taught me how complicated love can be.

This book is for you, Ed.
You taught me to trust love anyway.

CONTENTS

FOREWORD

There is a fascinating connection between stories about mythic quests and memoirs. The main characters in both forms of storytelling reveal to the reader how they encounter and survive, even transcend extraordinary ordeals. The more intriguing the struggle, the more fascinating the story.

This book was originally titled *Love Is Complicated.* These words hint at the book's dramatic narrative. The medieval roots of the deceptively simple word *complicate* originally meant "folded, confused, intricate." Three words that are at the heart of any engaging story because they suggest something is hidden that will be revealed, some darkness that will turn to light, a truth that will win out.

As author Mary Karr writes, the most moving memoirs are "the record of someone's honest struggle," and Fiol's book accomplishes that. She describes herself as the "horrible, rebellious daughter" of a father who was a living paradox, a selfless doctor working with lepers in Paraguay but also an "angry disciplinarian" who was so "clouded with fury" that he relentlessly beat her when she was a child.

Betrayal, abuse, and anger at God and the gods are the stuff of classical tragedy. What makes this account remarkable is how Fiol reveals the personal in the universal. Her bitter descriptions of the self-righteousness of the religious community she was raised in are balanced with rhapsodic scenes of singing in the choir. But the combination of resentment toward the violence at home and the hypocrisy at church take a toll then and later in life. The descriptions of her marriages and divorces, children, education, friendships and career are rendered as stages on a journey of reconciliation with her father—but also with herself.

This theme of mutual forgiveness is a powerful illustration of the venerable aphorism that those who cannot forgive and want to exact revenge might just as well dig two graves. Such is the corrosive power of bitterness, what I have to come to think of as "soul rust," the psychological acid that corrodes us from within. In this way, hers is a cautionary tale warning us about the dangers of the obstinate reluctance to forgive others and ourselves, which inevitably leads to anger, grief, and lovelessness.

Hence, the importance of Mother Teresa's inimitable advice, "People are often unreasonable, illogical, and self-centered; Forgive them *anyway*."

The value of this book, then, lies in the way the author recounts her *anyway*, her road to atonement—*at-one-ment*—or wholeness: her path from brokenness to healing.

The truth and beauty of mutual forgiveness are encapsulated in a ritual exchange between father and daughter after they made peace with each other.

"*Doa ess nuscht tsweschen ons*," Fiol's father would say to her in his native low German language. "There is nothing bad between us." And then she would repeat the words back to him.

This almost painfully beautiful exchange acknowledges that there may have been something wrong between us in the past, but not now, not in this one bountiful and *complicated* moment, not if we can find some good in the bad, some beauty in the terror.

Given the significance of these words to Marlena's reconciliation journey, *Nothing Bad Between Us* became the new title of this book.

Because Marlena Fiol, in her struggle for freedom, was able to make peace with her father and her faith, she reveals a path toward an accomplished and bitterfree life.

Hers is an epic journey of reconciliation.

—PHIL COUSINEAU

San Francisco 2020

Author of *Beyond Forgiveness: Reflections on Atonement*

PROLOGUE:
Unclean (1969–1970)

"When a person has...a case of leprous
disease...if the disease appears to be deeper
than the skin of his body...the priest...
shall pronounce him unclean."

—Leviticus 13:2–3

In the dark, squared-off pews of the German Mennonite church sanctuary sat my accusers, stern and silent, all eyes converging on me. I dropped my head and concentrated on the rectangular pattern of the tile floor. The closed church shutters kept out the fiery late afternoon Paraguay sun. The weight of the musty, trapped air was suffocating.

Pastor Arnold Entz, a short, balding man with stooped shoulders and a large belly stretching the seams of a black jacket a few sizes too small for him, ushered me in through a narrow door at the front of the church. We walked beside the choir platform where I stood to sing each Sunday and behind the organ that I had played for seven years, since I was eleven. A single, straight-backed, wooden chair had been placed next to the pulpit.

The pastor signaled for me to sit. I made my way to the chair without looking up. I had dressed judiciously for this meeting. My dark gray skirt hung well below my knees. My arms itched against the starched, long sleeves of my white shirt, buttoned neck-high. I had pulled my long, wild, reddish-brown hair into a tight bun at the nape of my neck. I wore no makeup.

Pastor Entz addressed the rows and rows of pews in High German. Although Mennonites in Paraguay all spoke the guttural, mostly unwritten *Plautdietsch* (Low German) to one another, in church we spoke only the more dignified High German, which was a distinctly different language. For example, "church excommunication" in *Plautdietsch* is "*Tjoatjebaun*" while in High German it is "*Kirchenverbot.*"

"We have called a special church meeting on this first Sunday in January to discuss your sins and to determine the consequences," Pastor Entz said, turning to me. Heavy silence. I swallowed hard to keep acid from rising in my throat.

•••

The regular church service earlier that day had been excruciating, although nothing out of the ordinary happened. I played the organ for fifteen minutes before the service began, watching people file in slowly and somberly. Men on the left, women on the right. The women, their hair in braids wrapped around their heads or in a tight bun, wore mostly white blouses and dark skirts. The men similarly wore dark pants and white shirts. They all sat with heads bent in devout and reverent silence.

My stomach burned and my fingers trembled, but I continued to play one magnificent hymn after another, like "*Lobe den Herren*" ("Praise Thou the Lord") and "*Wach auf Mein Herz*" ("Awake My Heart"). I knew most of them by heart. I loved these hymns. For me, they were the best part of being a Mennonite.

I kept thinking: *Are they eying me differently? What do they know about my transgressions?* In their view, even simple pleasures like listening to secular music or dancing were worldly and dangerous, for such entertainment dragged us down to the temptations of Satan. Women's clothing that was in the least bit immodest, showing a knee or too much of the neck or arms, was sinful because it caused men to lust. Just two months earlier, Pastor Entz had warned me that I was becoming too prideful about my mop of wild

Nothing Bad Between Us

reddish-brown hair and that I should either braid and wrap it around my head (like other good Mennonite women did) or cut it off so it wouldn't be a distraction for men.

I loved my long hair and refused to cut it, but for this day I had tied it up properly. My first inclination, as I stood in front of the mirror getting ready for church earlier that day, had been to leave it wild and untamed around my face and down my back. A final act of defiance in the face of my admission of defeat. But in the end, feelings of guilt and shame had overwhelmed the urge to defy.

I scanned the stern faces of the congregants entering the sanctuary, trying to determine what they knew about my sins. And almost on automatic, my fingers kept playing the glorious Mennonite hymns of grace, mercy, and love.

Pastor Entz signaled for me to begin playing the doxology, an invocation in praise of God that we all sang together at the start of each worship service. The solemn rows of people clad in black and white rose to their feet and swelled into four-part harmony.

> *Herr Gott, Dich loben alle wir*
> *Und sollen billig danken Dir...*
> Praise God, from whom all blessings flow,
> Praise Him all creatures here below...

The pastor rose to stand behind the pulpit. "God created man, sinless and holy. Then He subjected him to a moral test. Man yielded to the temptation of Satan."

Oh no, he's talking about sex again, I thought. I knew Hans and I had yielded to the temptation of Satan. How could it have felt so safe, so right, when it was so wrong?

He continued, a stern look on his face, "And by willfully disobeying God, man failed to maintain that holy condition in which he was created. By this act of disobedience, depravity and death were brought upon all of us. Although we have all inherited a sinful nature because of the sins of Adam and Eve, we are not guilty of their original act of disobedience. Those who perish in hell do so because of their own sins."

And today I will have to disclose my sins to this entire congregation.

"Sinners who are self-centered, self-willed, and rebellious toward God are unable to break the bondage of sin, and therefore will suffer under divine judgment." Pastor Entz's voice rose to a thunderous crescendo when he spoke those last words. The congregants, heads bent, nodded as though concurring, *Sinners be judged...*

The words were familiar. I had heard them many times before. But this time I flushed deeply because they seemed directed specifically at me. I was about to personally and publicly stand before that divine judgment.

When the service finally ended, I ran out of the church before anyone could approach me. The special meeting was to begin in just half an hour. Not knowing what else to do, I hid in the shade of a dark fern-leaved *paraíso* tree behind the church until I saw the pastor step out of the sanctuary, looking for me.

•••

Now I sat in front of my accusers. Pastor Entz's feet shifted uncomfortably as he put his weight on one foot and then the other at the front of the church. "You are aware of why we are all here this afternoon?"

I still kept my eyes on the floor. "I...I'm not sure," I replied in a shaky voice, swallowing again. Even without seeing the congregants, I felt their merciless eyes boring into me, and I sensed the energy of their heads shaking in disgust and disbelief. I wondered if my parents had come, but I didn't dare raise my head to search for them and meet their eyes.

"We have a witness who has submitted a claim that you have committed a serious offense against God and man. The congregation requests that you recount your transgressions. We will then decide what your punishment shall be."

I thought about how little this congregation knew or cared about what had really happened to me. A year prior, at age seventeen, I had been at the top of my high school class at the Liceo de San Carlos in Asunción, the capital city of Paraguay. I was strong and independent. I'd navigated life in the big city with little supervision since I was ten. My parents had founded and ran a leprosy compound located about an hour east of Asunción. While they were busy with the important work of healing sick bodies and saving lost souls, my brothers and sisters and I were shipped out to various locations to attend school. To get the attention and admiration I craved, I excelled at everything academic. I was a star student.

And then one night, Hans showed up on the streets of Asunción in his flashy red Chevy and my life began to unravel. His ostentatious car and flamboyant style stood out glaringly against the drab Mennonite canvas that had been my life. I found assurance in his car, his style, and most especially, in his attention to me. When he spoke to me, his voice was deep and gentle. His strong arms seemed to know just how much I needed to be held. In the circle of his arms, I felt secure.

I had known for a while that I would have to face the consequences of what I had done. A month earlier, Annaliese, a Mennonite nurse, had seen Hans visit me while I was in the *Hospital Bautista*. Curious about why he would have come to see me, she had checked my medical records:

Advanced gonorrhea. Pregnant. Father of the baby:
Hans Thiessen.

Annaliese's religious zeal to expose a sinner had apparently eradicated any medical vow of confidentiality, and she'd reported the medical details to Pastor Entz. The pastor had told me this when he came out to the leprosy station just before Christmas to inform me about this special meeting of the congregation. He'd informed me that the congregants were to meet about this matter after our regular church service the first Sunday of the new year, the 4th of January.

I knew the pastor had told my folks about the meeting. But I didn't bring it up with them, and for the next few weeks at home they said nothing to me about it. I did, however, overhear them talking about it in their bedroom, late one night.

"John, if we sit there in that church, people will look at us like we're the cause of Marlena's sinfulness," Mom said. "They'll condemn us right along with her. It will destroy everything we've worked so hard for, this leprosy work—God's work."

"It'll destroy it whether we're there or not," Dad said in a steady cold voice.

"I just wish none of it had ever happened." Mom's sobs sounded as though she was burying her face in a pillow.

"Well, it did. And we have to face up to it," he said.

I waited for something more, but their conversation ended. As I got ready for bed, a heavy mass lodged itself deep inside my chest. There was nothing surprising to me about what I heard my parents say. It was a given in our family that God's work naturally took precedence over everything else. Still, I longed to hear some small hint that they cared about me, even after all I had done.

•••

The pastor's voice brought me back to the present. "Please recount your transgressions, Marlena."

"I… I…" I couldn't mouth the words.

My chest muscles seemed to pull themselves into a tight knot. The scar on my belly began to throb, not yet healed from surgery the previous month. The gash felt like hot barbed wire running from my navel to my pelvis. I pushed my clenched fists hard against my lower abdomen to keep it from exploding with pain.

Pastor Entz impatiently cleared his throat. "Did you have adulterous sexual relations with Hans, knowing that he was married?" he tried again. A weighty silence fell on the sanctuary as the congregants awaited my response.

"Ja," I said and nodded without looking up.

A low murmur rippled through the sanctuary. The pastor turned to face the congregation like a judge turning toward the jury, inviting them to join in the enquiry.

"How long did you flaunt and expose your body to this married man?" I recognized the voice of David Reimer in the second row. I didn't know him well, but he always sat near the front of the church and I had often caught him gawking at my legs when I played the organ.

"About one year," I answered to the floor, pressing my thighs and knees even more tightly together. Actually, it had been eleven months and five days.

The questions continued from other attendees.

"How often did you engage in this sinful behavior?" "How did you get away with it for so long?" "Why didn't you understand the sin you were committing?" "Whom else did you have sex with?" "When did you contract the venereal disease?" After a while my head began to spin and I answered the barrage of questions as if I were speaking about someone else.

Finally, the pastor stepped forward as though to signal a conclusion to this part of the meeting. He turned to me. "Have you fully terminated this adulterous and sinful behavior, and do you vow before God and this congregation that you will never again walk down that sinful path?"

Never again? Hans and I had ended our sinful behavior. But never again? What did that mean? Never again to feel a man's arms around me, his weight against me? Or never again to consort with someone who already had a wife?

Suddenly I panicked, wondering again if my parents were in the congregation, listening to all of this. My hunched shoulders bent down even farther. Almost in a whisper, I said, "Ja."

The pastor led me out of the main sanctuary. He left me in the small vestibule on the side and returned to the sanctuary to lead the discussion about what to do with me.

I could hear the sound of their voices, sometimes multiple voices on top of one another. From where I sat, it sounded like they were all competing to give expression to the monstrous thing I had done. I caught a few words when a woman's voice cried out above the others, "She always did act like..." but I couldn't make out the rest.

What were they going to do to me? I knew that the Commission for Congregational Concerns, which included the church I belonged to, had ruled that young women who had consummated sexual relations prior to marriage should symbolize this at their wedding by not wearing a headdress and veil. This reflected the long, severe history of disciplining sexual offenses among the Russian Mennonites who had immigrated to Paraguay. All through the history of the Mennonite church, no sin is attacked more severely than the sexual transgressions of women. Men got off more easily. For me to have committed this most serious of offenses with a married man was beyond any official ruling. I didn't really care much about Mennonite doctrine, but I loved making music in my church. Would I have to give up all that because of what I had done?

My hands rested protectively over the throbbing scar on my lower abdomen. I recalled the moment I had awakened from my surgery a month ago. "There is more, so much more than you people know anything about," I whispered under my breath.

The door creaked open. Without a word, the pastor led me back to my chair.

Slowly, I pulled my eyes up off the floor and stared out across the stony faces. There were hundreds of them. They were nothing but a blur until my eyes fell on my father. He sat alone, without my mother, near the door at the very back of the church. His shoulders were squared and his chin was up. The rigidity of his straight back was formidable. He didn't flinch, just stared at me coldly, hands clasped in his lap. My dad was always clear about what was right and wrong before God. And he tolerated no wrongs.

Tearing my eyes away from my father, I saw Heinz Duerksen and Hans Penner (both on the Mennonite administrative committee charged with overseeing Dad's leprosy station) just two rows up and to Dad's left. They glanced at each other and, solemnly shaking their heads, looked back to where my father sat. My father had given himself completely to the treatment of leprosy in Paraguay. He was a hero in the eyes of the people in this congregation—or rather, I thought in dismay, he had been a hero before I brought him shame.

I wanted to flee. But guilt kept me glued to the chair. The congregants looked satisfied with themselves, as though they had just successfully completed an important task.

It was unanimous.

"You are no longer allowed to sing in the choir or play the organ for Sunday services," announced the pastor in a monotone, turning toward me, his large belly protruding with authority. "Now, let us pray."

"*Lieber Vater im Himmel, wir danken Dir für Deine Gnade...* Dear Father in heaven, we thank you for your grace..." His voice droned on and on.

Nothing Bad Between Us

I heard nothing further. They had just taken away from me all that I held most dear about the Mennonite church. I loved the music. But it wasn't just that. I had been a soloist in the choir and the church leaders consistently had shown such appreciation for my organ playing.

How was I supposed to face these people now? I imagined the word *UNCLEAN* stamped in red letters on my forehead.

The prayer finally ended and people rose to leave. I watched my father's rigid back as he strode out and disappeared.

CHAPTER 1:
The Lord's Work (1941–1960)

My father in 1941

———

*"The reasonable man adapts himself to the
world: the unreasonable one persists in trying
to adapt the world to himself. Therefore, all
progress depends on the unreasonable man."*

—George Bernard Shaw

———

My father was an unreasonable man. In 1941, just out of medical school, he
gave up the possibility of a lucrative practice in the US to serve as a doctor for a
newly established German Mennonite colony in Paraguay. These Mennonites
had recently emigrated from Russia to a barren region in the western part
of Paraguay, South America, called the Chaco, at the time considered a land
where no white man could live.

I often heard stories about those years in the Chaco. My dad's medical
books didn't arrive until well into his first year there. For two years, in a one-
room thatched-roofed hut with hard mud floors and without a nurse, he
performed surgeries he hadn't been trained to perform and treated diseases
he'd never heard of. The fiery young Mennonite doctor knew this was the
Lord's will, so he did whatever it took to carry it out. He built his surgical

team with what he had. For his anesthetist, he trained a grade school teacher. For IV fluids, he set up a crude still to make distilled water from collected rainwater. For iron, he went to the blacksmith and heated rusted iron red hot. Then he ground it up in a mortar and pestle and had people ingest it to treat anemia, a common problem because of hookworm infections.

But when the long day's work was done and he lay alone on his straw-filled mattress at night, my father's mind wandered to what it would be like to have a trained nurse by his side. And a wife. He thought about the shy young nurse in Kansas his brother Herb had introduced him to just the day before leaving for Paraguay. He remembered her name, Clara Regier, and that she came from good Mennonite stock. He also recalled her clear blue eyes and full lips. During those long, lonely nights in the Chaco, he thought about Clara and wondered if she might be the one the Lord had chosen for him.

I still have the letter he wrote to my mother Clara, which took three months to get to her. It read:

> Before I left the US to come to Paraguay, I felt the need to look for a life partner. Since my interest was to find a Mennonite girl, I asked my brother Herb to look out for one in Kansas. So this is what he did. He helped me get acquainted with you. I have a special purpose in mind for this letter. Especially at my age of thirty years, it must be obvious to you what interest I have in our correspondence...

They were engaged by mail. My mom had dedicated her life to serve the Lord when she was just a young girl at a revival camp. Through my father's ardent and God-filled letters, she came to believe that joining him was the Lord's calling. After a year and a half, Dad returned to the US to marry her and together they returned to the Chaco of west Paraguay. They had been in the Chaco for almost three years when Dad developed bloody stools. His self-diagnosis was a bleeding ulcer. My mother put him to bed, where he remained for weeks, feeling feeble and useless.

This time, it was the doctor who needed medical care, and there was none. So my parents requested a replacement and made plans to leave. Their honeymoon had ended. They returned to the States with their two children, John Junior and Elisabeth. Wesley, their third, was on the way. As far as they were concerned, their service in South America had ended and they were ready to settle down in the US with their growing family.

My father established a successful medical practice in a Mennonite farming community in the Midwest. He and my mother tasted the American dream life, complete with a fourth child, a little white house with blue shutters, a picket fence, and even a car. But during those five years of abundance, they felt a growing disorientation, even depression, perceiving an ever-widening gap between the comfortable life they were living and the life of service to the Lord they thought they were called to live.

That was all about to change.

The Mennonite Central Committee (MCC) became aware of the need for leprosy treatment in Paraguay through its involvement with the Mennonites who had settled in the Chaco colonies. The plan was to build a leper colony in east Paraguay, where the disease was considered to be rampant. Now MCC needed a doctor to head up the project. My father's training and familiarity with the country made him a prime candidate.

I loved hearing my folks tell the story about how they made this life-changing decision.

One snowy Saturday morning in early March, Dad walked into the kitchen where my very-pregnant-with-me mother stood over a hot stove. "Clara, can you quit doing that for a minute? We need to talk."

"What is it, John?"

"Do you remember the committee I was on in Paraguay before we came back to the States? The one that MCC formed to investigate the possibility of founding a leprosy colony in east Paraguay?" he asked.

"I do," she said. "Why do you ask?" Mom told me years later how my dad's eyes blazed as though they were on fire that day, like she hadn't seen in years.

"Well, MCC is planning to move forward with the leprosy project. They sent us a letter asking if we'd consider going back..."

"What are you saying, John?" She interrupted him.

"I'm saying, I think we are being called to go back to Paraguay."

My parents used the word "called" to explain all of their major life decisions. If they were called to do something, they were compelled to do it by a powerful God-force working through them.

"God is giving us another chance to do something important, to do something that actually matters," he said.

"But John, I've always heard that leprosy is such a mysterious condition that we know very little about. It's even associated with some type of curse, which is why lepers are most often isolated and ostracized, and there's no cure for the disease." The words tumbled out of her. "How would we be able to help them?"

"We'll find a way if this is what the Lord wants us to do," he said.

"But it's highly contagious. What about our children? What about this baby in my belly?"

"Clara, we must remember what the Lord said to Jacob in the Bible: Don't be afraid, for I will protect you." I can imagine that by then my dad was staring out the window, that faraway look in his eyes, already plotting their next adventure.

•••

Less than six months after that conversation, our family boarded the *SS Brazil* on our way to Paraguay. On August 23, 1951, the *SS Brazil* sailed out of the harbor in New York. It was a huge vessel for the times, with cabins for 359 first-class and 160 tourist-class passengers. Among the latter were my parents, with five children under the age of seven. I was the youngest, just one day shy of four months.

Years later, I asked my mother about that trip.

"I was terrified that the older four children would get lost," she said, "so I made cardboard signs with each child's name and hung them around their necks. We stowed you away in a portable buggy."

"What were your rooms like on the ship?" I asked, already knowing they were in the lowest-class cabins.

"The seven of us were crammed into two tourist-class cabins, the boys and Daddy in one, you girls and me in the other," she said. "Each cabin had a little rusty sink off in one corner. First-class passengers got laundry facilities, but not us."

"It smelled like we were living in a toilet," she added. "There was hardly any soap and you children all had diarrhea. I couldn't possibly keep up with all of the dirty diapers and underwear in that little sink. And there was no place to hang it all."

"Did you ever regret your decision and wish you could turn back?" I asked.

"Oh, sometimes I grumbled because it just felt like too much. But you know Daddy. He didn't have much patience for complaints. "Stop *diene Kloage*—your complaints," he'd say to me. "This is not about us. It's about the Lord's work."

"And, of course, he was right," she added, smiling. "We arrived in Asunción after more than a month, a dirty, bedraggled, emaciated, and exhausted group. But when Daddy and I stepped off that boat and looked out over the ancient city that lay in front of us, we knew we were where we were supposed to be and were just thankful that God had protected us."

•••

Asunción, the capital city of Paraguay, sits on the left bank of the *Rio Paraguay*, almost at the confluence of this river and the *Rio Pilcomayo*. The city spreads out over gentle hills in a pattern of rectangular blocks, covered by a sea of red-tiled roofs. The streets are smooth, worn cobblestones lined with paraíso trees, their yellow fruit spread around them on the ground. With Moorish architectural features brought from Spain in the sixteenth century, the houses stand hard and impenetrable by the street, offering the passersby cold walls with shuttered French doors opening onto balconies high above the street.

Peter Wiens, a short young man with wire-rimmed glasses, was the Mennonite delegate who was there to meet us. He had brought a car to take us to the apartment he had rented for us in the city. We would live there while my parents planned and built the leprosy station eighty-one kilometers (about fifty miles) to the east.

My folks have described to me how Wiens was about to turn into a side street but abruptly stopped. Just a short block in front of them, they could see that the cross street had become a flood, carrying dead branches, broken plastic bottles, tattered pieces of clothing, rotted produce, and feces. A bus was stalled at the intersection in the deep murky water, and pedestrians were unable to cross the street, which looked like a swollen river.

Wiens made a sharp turn away from the torrent and explained that the city had no water system and no sewage disposal system. All the garbage on the street was carried away during showers by the floods of water along streets sloping toward the river.

Eventually, he stopped the car in front of an imposing, dark outer wall. "This is your new home," he said.

•••

Eighty-one kilometers east of Asunción stands a kilometer marker that simply reads "Kilómetro 81," which became the name of the leprosy station: *Hospital Menonita* at *Kilómetro Ochenta y Uno*. The marker stands beside the *Ruta*, a narrow two-lane highway that runs from Asunción to the Brazilian border. Cars and buses, overloaded with masses of people and animals bulging from their windows and doors, share the *Ruta* with ox-drawn carts and straight-backed women walking alongside the road, their goods balanced on their heads like the crowns of goddesses.

My parents spent most of the next two years designing and building the leprosy station at Km. 81. They were once again doing adventuresome and important work, the Lord's work, and nothing could stop them. Sometimes they would stay out there for days at a time, sleeping in makeshift tents and eating whatever rations they had taken out with them. "Helpers" from the Chaco German Mennonite colonies came to Asunción to stay with us kids, and others went farther east to help construct the first buildings at Km. 81. That's what my folks called them, God's Helpers.

My parents were often late to catch the bus and had to rush to get out of our apartment. My mother described for me later how we little ones tugged at her skirt. "Momma, please don't go." But my mother pushed us gently aside and took her place beside her doctor-husband, doing the work they were called to do.

Together they oversaw the clearing of the land. With only a few Paraguayan and German Mennonite workers helping them, they plowed the ground and planted trees: orange, tangerine, grapefruit, loquat, avocado, *guayaba*, and mulberry. My father personally drew the architectural plans. He oversaw the construction of the hospital, the buildings to house the most critically ill leprosy patients, our family home, and the homes for the many people who eventually joined him in running the station, mostly Mennonites from the Chaco in west Paraguay.

He considered the service of God's Helpers at the station a form of giving back to Paraguay for what the country's leaders had offered these Russian immigrants when no other country would give them the military exemption and religious freedoms they requested. He often said, "The most important function of the leprosy station is to provide an opportunity for us Mennonites to give back to Paraguay."

•••

Years later, Dad told me about those early experiences. One cold stormy night in July, he was out looking for patients. He guided his horse toward a mud-walled shack with a threadbare thatched roof. Neighbors farther up the road had known nothing about anyone with a skin problem, but they had told him that Juan, who lived in this house, was sick with a high fever.

Through the open doorway, he saw a kerosene lamp on a broken-down wooden table near the center of the single room of the shack. In a back corner on a rough cornhusk mattress lay a man partly covered with a thin tattered blanket. A sleeping child lay next to him. A young woman, her black hair in a long braid down her back, was bending over them.

Dad stepped through the doorway and abruptly backed up as a pungent odor assaulted him.

"*Soy un doctor*," he said, his right hand covering his nose.

"*Doctor*," the woman said, "my man is burning up with fever and there's something wrong with his foot, but he keeps saying nothing hurts."

"Let's take a look at it," Dad said.

Juan's foot was purple and swollen. Foul-smelling brownish pus was oozing from an open wound and had pooled onto the mattress.

After Juan's wife got him to the station in their ox-drawn cart and after his foot and fever were treated, my father introduced him to the small group of critically ill patients living at our leprosy station. He wanted Juan and his wife to learn about his disease from their own people.

The first person they met had no eyebrows and his nose was a caved-in bridge. His ears were covered with lumps. Sitting near him was an elderly woman, completely blind and missing most of her fingers. Another patient was missing a leg.

It was soon clear to the new patient what kind of threat he faced. My father calmly explained that leprosy probably wasn't inherited or spread through skin contact. He thought it was likely transmitted through the nose or mouth. He believed they'd be fine on medications at home with their family.

Dad always insisted that patients with leprosy not be ostracized and removed from their homes unless they were too ill to survive on their own. He revolutionized how leprosy was, and currently is, treated on the planet.

•••

The day before my second birthday, we moved to Km. 81. Our house wasn't nearly finished, but we had to vacate our rented apartment in Asunción, so my folks made the decision to move the whole family out to the station. The tile roof and the red brick outer walls were up, but there were no windows or doors. During the cold, rainy winter months that followed, we had to wear several layers of jackets in bed to stay warm.

That's where I grew up, among the sickest of the sick leprosy patients. In fact, early on, my parents sometimes saw patients in our unfinished home, using our beds as examining tables. The patients were part of our extended family.

We attended school on the leprosy station grounds with fifteen other students, children of the Helpers from the Chaco of west Paraguay. The one-room German school housed kindergarten to third grade classes. After third grade, we kids took correspondence courses or were shipped elsewhere to continue our education.

Our parents often asked us kids to sing hymns for the patients who lived at the station. I loved to sing, so that was no hardship for me. One night after singing, I lingered at the open doorway of *Doña Ramona*'s one-room shack. I was only nine, and *Doña Ramona* had been really old as long as I'd known her. She was one of the first patients to live on our station after her family abandoned her. When she came, she was covered with pus sores, she was blind, her nose and ear cartilage was broken down, and her extremities were bloody stumps. After coming to live with us, she was still blind, her cartilage was still caved in, and she had permanently lost most of her toes and fingers. But she smiled a lot.

She sat on the dirt floor in the center of her hut next to the red-hot coals from an earlier fire. Sensing my presence, she turned toward the doorway. "*Sí...?*" Her voice rose into a question.

"*Doña Ramona, soy* Marlena," I said, hesitatingly moving in toward her.

"Thank you for singing," she said in Spanish, her wrinkled, sunken, dark face breaking into a smile.

She seemed so ancient and so wise. I wanted to talk to her, wanted to know why she was always happy. But we spoke German on the station, so I understood almost no Spanish. Besides, as much as I was drawn to her, she also repulsed me, with that creepy broken-down face. I turned and ran from her place and didn't stop running until I got to our house. I shut myself into the girls' bedroom and threw myself facedown on my narrow, hard bed. Deep down, I longed to be a good Mennonite who could love these people the way my mom did, always holding their hands and wiping their foreheads. And just as deep down, I screamed to get away from it all.

•••

I know my mother was sometimes concerned about the risks of raising us kids on the station. I remember one evening in particular, not long after my visit with *Doña Ramona*, when I overheard my parents talking in low voices to each other in their bedroom. "We don't even know for sure how leprosy is spread. Do you think we're putting our family at risk, our children, here, in the midst of these patients?" My mother's voice was heavy with anxiety.

"*Waut sajst Du*?" Dad often reverted to Low German whenever he was upset. "Are you saying that you want to run home to your mother? We have work to do here. The Lord has called us to do His work. Now let's get some sleep."

I thought about *Doña Ramona*.

A shiver ran down the edge of my spine and I shuddered. *Was Mom saying that I might look like her if I hung out with the patients? So why did Mom and Dad always ask me to go sing for them? Did they even care?*

As I made my way across the veranda to the girls' bedroom, I clenched my teeth together hard to keep from screaming. *Who was this Lord God of theirs that was so important, more important than anything else?* I wanted to pummel that Lord, pound on him, make him disappear. But I didn't know how. And I immediately felt guilty about having such evil thoughts about God.

•••

Us contracting leprosy was only one of the many risks my parents took during those years. My mother once described to us something that happened to her on a steamy hot afternoon when Dad was out on one of his searches for patients.

Mom had finished whitewashing a wall of the new brick station kitchen and sat exhausted against a tree, fanning herself. A truck pulled into the station grounds. She quickly rose when she saw a half dozen or so young Paraguayan men in the bed of the truck, fists in the air, yelling something she couldn't understand.

She called out to Francisco, the bricklayer working near her, "Francisco, what are they saying? What's going on?" She began to back up when she saw a few of the young men jump off the back of the truck, still shouting.

"They're from *Itacurubí*, and they're shouting that you will not live and that they will destroy this property unless you leave. They don't want lepers in their neighborhood."

The men reached up into the truck and began to pull out large rocks. Francisco continued, "They're saying that they've brought these rocks to destroy you and your satanic work."

Mom told us how her hands began to shake. She wished she knew how to speak Spanish. Surely she could explain the Lord's work if she did.

After some moments of hesitation, she turned back to Francisco. "Please ask them if they would like to have some coffee and *Zwieback* [a Russian Mennonite bread]. I think I also have some cookies," she said.

Francisco relayed the message. The men stopped shouting. Still grasping their rocks, they looked at her in silent disbelief. The driver of the truck and *jefe* of the operation said something to the men, and they dropped their rocks.

Never taking her eyes off them, my mother moved toward the lean-to where she kept what little provisions she had brought out from the city. "Here, I have this thermos full of iced coffee and these are *Zwieback* that our helper in Asunción baked just yesterday. You probably don't know what *Zwieback* are..." In her nervousness she forgot that they didn't understand a word she was saying. "Um... Francisco, can you please tell them I'd like to pray with them before we eat?"

The men stood awkwardly near the truck as though not trusting this strange white woman who offered food and wanted to pray with them after hearing that they were here to kill her and destroy her property.

Mom said she clasped her trembling hands together. "Lord, we thank you for your love and protection. Bless this food, we pray, in Christ's name. Amen." She held out the bag of *Zwieback* and motioned for the men to come.

They ate *Zwieback* and drank iced coffee with my mother and then quietly left. They never returned.

•••

Not long after that angry encounter, Dad stormed into the house waving a letter at my mother, who stood at the kerosene stove cooking rice with warm milk and cinnamon for our supper. I was setting the table on the veranda and could see them through the kitchen window.

"Clara, I can't believe this! Look at this letter." His angry voice reverberated off the newly tiled floor.

I sank into a chair. It was always so scary when Dad became highly upset, even if it wasn't directed toward me.

The letter was from the American Leprosy Mission (ALM) in the US, one of the key financial supporters of the leprosy station. Mom began to read, looking up to search his face after reading out loud the part that said, *we have no choice but to withhold funding*...

Dad interrupted her reading. "Even after I've proved to them that the patients are out there and that most of them are able to stay in their homes as long as they're on their medications, MCC and ALM continue to criticize my approach, and now they're telling us they'll no longer support the work." He began stomping around the kitchen. "I'm more convinced than ever that ambulatory treatment is the way to go. But they can think only in terms of a traditional leper colony."

"John..." she began.

He again interrupted her. "And what happened to you when those men from *Itacurubí* came with their truck full of rocks? That's just one more reason why we shouldn't be building a leper colony here. They just don't understand."

"John, please lower your voice. We don't want to scare the children," my mother said, folding the letter in her lap. She was silent for a moment. "Let's help them understand. Let's write a long letter inviting MCC and ALM representatives to come check it out for themselves—to come see how well it's working."

I was only nine and didn't know much about MCC or ALM. But I wasn't at all sure I was on my dad's side on this. Secretly, I wished they would shut down the station so we could just have a normal family like everyone else.

In the end, Dad had his way. Almost two decades later, O. W. Hasselblad, who was then president of the American Leprosy Mission and well acquainted with the treatment of leprosy worldwide, published this statement:

> *The spirit of cooperation between the Government of Paraguay, the Mennonite Central Committee, and the American Leprosy Mission has permitted the work of Kilometer 81 to become a fine example of a successful program of leprosy control. Three elements are essential in such a first-rate program. One is domiciliary treatment of a patient. So far as I know, John*

Schmidt was the first to try such a program any place in the world. That was a courageous and pioneering venture, and it has become the basis for leprosy control work throughout the world today. It virtually eliminates the need for the "settlements" of several decades ago.

As I write this, over 180,000 people worldwide are infected with leprosy, according to the World Health Organization. Today, most countries follow my father's revolutionary model of integrating leprosy services into general health services, rather than ostracizing leprosy patients.

Experts now say that leprosy is actually not as contagious as once thought. You can catch it only if you come into repeated contact with nose and mouth fluids from someone with the disease, and you must have a genetic predisposition to get it.

None of us ever contracted the disease.

CHAPTER 2:
11,187 Miles by Volvo (1960)

Pushing our Volvo over the Andes

———

"...there ain't no journey what
don't change you some."

—David Mitchell, *Cloud Atlas*

———

"There it is." Dad pointed to the ferry that was docked in the bay of the *Río Paraguay*. His eyes followed the heavy cranes that lifted a small gray station wagon from the ferry and dropped it on the dock as though it were a toy. "That's our Volvo."

We were all there, Mom and Dad and all six of us kids lined up on the dock. I had never seen my father so excited. On the way over here, he had almost run over an oxcart piled high with sacks of some sort, which had been crawling along on the side of the *Ruta*. And as soon as he parked the Km. 81 station wagon near the dock, Dad had run ahead of us to get the first glimpse of the Volvo he had ordered from Sweden.

I wasn't very interested in the car. And I couldn't figure out why this was all such a big deal to my father. For many months, he had shut himself into his office in the evenings, poring through piles and piles of papers.

One evening I asked my mother about it.

"It's our big trip," she said. "It's a trip Daddy has dreamed about since coming to Paraguay. We've found another doctor who will care for the patients while we're gone. We're going to drive all the way from Paraguay to the States. He's working on getting all the visas and other paperwork that are needed."

"Is there really a road that goes all the way from Paraguay to the States?" I asked.

"Yes, there is," she said. "It's called the Pan-American Highway."

Pan-American sounded so sophisticated. I imagined a smooth, wide superhighway, like pictures I had seen in magazines from the US.

The Pan-American Highway is actually not a single highway, but rather a network of roads measuring about 48,000 kilometers (about 30,000 miles) in total length from Chile to Alaska. The road connects almost all of the countries of South, Central, and North America. According to *Guinness World Records*, the Pan-American Highway is the world's longest "motorable road"—a designation that was laughable, really, in 1960. At times, the road was little more than a rutted dirt road or a steep gash through treacherous mountain passes. At other times, it ended at the banks of rivers with no drivable way to get across.

But here I stood, watching Dad's beloved Volvo make its Paraguayan debut, still believing there was a superhighway that would take us all the way to the States. My three older brothers ran along the dock, animatedly discussing the car's details with my father. "Look, it has a huge rear window." "Wow, Dad, it's much higher than it is wide." "How long did it take for it to get here from Sweden?"

I stared at them and frowned. Dad was acting like a kid. I had never seen him like this. I knew we were going to the States to do lots of talks and raise money for the leprosy mission. But this car and this idea about driving all the way to the States on the Pan-American superhighway didn't seem like very serious God-work.

•••

On the cold, drizzly morning of May 23, 1960, the Volvo was loaded down and we were ready to go. Volvo station wagons in 1960 looked nothing like they do today; it was boxy, top heavy and narrow. Dad had built a wooden rack behind the back seat of the car, under which my parents had packed provisions, clothes, and blankets. On the side of the gray Volvo, he had painted in large black lettering "*Lucha Antileprosa en el Paraguay*," ("Fight Against Leprosy in Paraguay") and underneath that, "*Misión Menonita.*" It was totally embarrassing. Everybody we met along the way would know that we came from a leprosy mission and that we were Mennonites.

"This is it. It's time to go," Dad proclaimed, his eyes flashing. He scooped three-year-old Mary Lou into his arms and tucked her into the back of the vehicle in the small space above the wooden rack, along with her *tuppi* (potty) for her constant carsickness. "You three, you're next, in there." He pointed to the middle of the back seat, next to my mom, who was already in the back seat by the window. I slid in next to her and my fat, red-faced brother and older sister pushed their way onto the seat beside me. My two oldest brothers sat proudly next to Dad in the front seat, turning knobs and fiddling with gadgets on the dashboard.

"I can't breathe in here," I complained, prying my body loose from David and my mother next to me and leaning forward toward the front of the car. "Why don't the back windows roll down in this stupid car?"

"*Hault diene Kloage*—stop your complaining, Marlena," Dad said, as he practically jumped into the seat behind the wheel. With a wide grin on his face, he turned back toward us. "Let's pray for the Lord's blessing on this journey."

And we were on our way. We drove to the ferry in Rosario to cross the *Paraná River* at the Paraguay-Argentina border. There we picked up Argentina National Route 11, a rough dirt road with no signage.

My mother pulled out her Remington typewriter, balanced it on her lap, and began to type: *It is not easy to drive here. So many times one doesn't know the way, there are few signs, and often people misdirect us, though they don't mean to...* Every time she got to the end of a line, her arm would jab me in the ribs as she pushed the carriage return back.

The first night we stopped at about five o'clock to set up camp next to a police station. We ate pea soup that Mom made by mixing water with dried soup mix. It tasted like salty water. Our homemade tent attached to the car's luggage rack at one end and sloped down to the ground on the other. Dad and the boys slept under the tent. Mom and we girls slept in the car, scrunched up on the seats.

I was cold, stiff, and cranky when Dad woke us up to get going at four thirty the next morning. Mom pulled out her small kerosene Primus stove and cooked instant cream of wheat. I took a bite and spit it out. It was undercooked and gritty between my chattering teeth.

"*Dit's eklich*—this is disgusting." I began to cry. Mary Lou was already crying and shaking from the cold.

"Take those two crybabies and put them in the back of the car," Dad said angrily.

I tried to keep my little sister warm in the back cubby of the car, while I watched the rest of them eating the gritty cereal and enduring Dad's long, earnest morning prayers.

•••

Like all good Mennonites, Dad had contacted the leaders of many missions and churches he knew of along the way before we left, and I think we must have visited them all, as well as missions they hadn't known of before we left. Many of the missionaries called special church meetings in honor of our visit. My folks delivered presentations about God's work in Paraguay, always with lots of slides. And to really top it all off, Mom and Dad lined up all six of us kids to sing "Jesus Loves Me" in German, English, and Spanish. Sometimes I didn't know which was worse: being in that car or with those missionaries.

One day, we drove into a small village in Bolivia. The road was dusty. The huts on either side were made of mud with thatched roofs and hard-packed dirt floors that one could see through the open doorways. Children, mostly naked, ran out onto the road as we drove in. Dirty, mangy dogs, tails between their legs, lurked about. Small groups of men in undershirts and baggy pants sat around playing cards. And women came and went, staring at us, carrying baskets of produce, bread, or other items on their heads.

Dad stopped the car and walked over to a group of men. "Are there any *misioneros* in town?"

The men stared at him. One of them rose. "*Sí. Algunos misioneros viven allí,*" he said, pointing back to where we had come from.

We thanked him and turned around but found no church or sign of a mission. Following another series of directions, we finally made our way to a little church on the other side of town. Dad walked up to the door of the hut that stood next to the church and rapped on the door.

A very pregnant white woman cautiously opened the door. "Yes?" she asked politely.

"We're missionaries from Paraguay, driving through, on our way to the States," he said. "Can we stay for the evening meal and the night? We can sleep on your church benches," he added, hopeful.

We sat in the car, watching, completely still. Wesley whispered from the front seat, "What if she doesn't let us stay? What do we do then? Do we have any food, Mom?"

I frowned. I didn't want to eat one more meal in another person's house, a person who felt obligated to feed us because we were missionaries. Or to sleep one more night on another person's church bench. I wanted to hide underneath the wooden rack in the back of the car.

We watched the woman hesitate, but then the Christian spirit seemingly moved her to nod. "Of course, come on in." Dad gestured to us and we all tumbled out of the car, stinky, sweaty, and starving.

Her mouth dropped open and her eyes widened. "How many are you?" she exclaimed, as she watched more and more of us dirty children of all ages piling out of the little Volvo.

"Meet my family," Dad said.

"God will Provide" was Dad's motto in life. My parents lived by that motto, and they believed other Christians lived by it as well. Mom and Dad took many hundreds of people into our home at the leprosy station over the years. They ate our food, slept in our beds, and received whatever they needed that my folks could provide. Their belief that Christians are the vehicles through which God will provide was a profound reflection of their absolute conviction that we are all here on earth to serve each other.

When we reached the Bolivian Andes, the dirt roads deteriorated into steep, treacherous, and narrow spirals. It seemed like we were always on the precipice side of the road when we passed trucks or buses coming the opposite direction. All of us would lean left into the middle of the road, as though we could shift the weight of the car and keep it from tumbling off the cliffs.

That morning, we finished our gritty cereal, suffered through Dad's long prayers, and were continuing the long climb into the Andes. As we crawled up in low gear, the Volvo ground to a halt. From where I sat, the car seemed to be pointing vertically up to the sky.

"You'll all have to get out and push," Dad said, pulling up hard on the hand brake to keep from rolling back and off the cliff behind us.

"This'll be fun," I said, stretching my cramped limbs. All of us except Mary Lou lined up behind the car and pushed. And pushed. The exhaust burned our noses and stung in our eyes as the car, with our weight no longer in it, slowly coughed its way forward. This became a familiar scene as, day after day, we pushed that car over the Andes.

Once the car began to get some traction, Dad kept driving as far as he could. We trudged up behind him. The deserted road ahead of us wound its way around curve after steep curve. Eventually, the Volvo was nowhere in sight. I lagged behind the rest. I felt dizzy, I couldn't breathe, and my legs buckled under my weight.

"*Etj goh nijch wieda*—I'm not going any further," I said, dropping to the ground in the middle of the road.

"Still having fun?" David taunted, looking back.

I watched them walk away from me, all of them. *Are they going to just leave me here, in these awful Bolivian mountains?* I groaned, as I pulled myself up off the ground to follow.

Finally, after crossing a high suspension bridge that spanned two towering passes, we caught sight of the Volvo. Dad stood beside the car, holding his head in his hands. "Time to push again," he said without looking up.

"John, what's wrong?" My mother put her hand on his shoulder.

He threw off her hand. "I have a migraine headache. I just want you all to keep quiet and push," he said.

Without a word, we all lined up behind the Volvo and pushed until the car again gained some traction and took off on its own. The next time we made our way toward it, I saw Dad retching on the side of the deep precipice.

Dad often suffered from migraine headaches at that high Andean altitude. When he felt one coming on, we all grew quiet and tense. We weren't allowed to make any noise. And when he vomited at the end of each bout, none of us got to eat until his stomach settled down.

•••

"It's time to move." Dad was always in a huge rush to get started before the sun was up.

We were in the dry, mountainous Bolivian village of Totora. The roads were dusty with very sparse vegetation along the sides. We had spent the night, fully dressed because it was so cold, on straw-filled sacks spread out on the concrete floor of a missionary's warehouse.

I groaned and pulled a sack over my head.

"Marlena, we don't have time for your nonsense this morning." Dad's voice had that edge that meant I would get no more warnings. As I sleepily dragged my sack to stack it up against the warehouse wall, I overheard my mother. "What are we going to do about our plan to go to Santa Cruz?"

"We're going to go," Dad said.

"But John, the pastor last night told us..." She lowered her voice. "John, he told us that road is only used by mules, and, because of the elections, there are likely to be bandits in that part of the country."

Now wide-awake, I asked, "Bandits? Where are the bandits?"

"Never mind," Dad said, glaring at me. "Now come on, let's get moving."

We all piled into the car. "What about breakfast?" I grumbled.

"We have no time for breakfast. We have a long, difficult road ahead to Santa Cruz," Dad said. "You can eat some of the leftover bread from yesterday."

Mom pulled the bit of bread from our food box behind her seat. It smelled stale and I saw that mold had begun to form around the crust.

"Maybe we don't need to eat right now," she said, quickly covering the food box so the musty smell wouldn't permeate the car.

My father leaned forward in his seat, eyes focused on the narrow dirt road in front of us, his white knuckles gripping the steering wheel. Whenever Dad looked like that, we didn't mess around. We all sat tense and quiet, forgetting our usual bickering about who was invading whose space.

After several hours, we approached the town of Alquile. The dusty dirt road, the mud-packed, broken-down houses with thatched roofs, and the brown landscape beyond all looked to me like I was seeing them through a lens that turned everything the same monotone shade of dirty brown.

Dad stopped the car at an outdoor market.

"Stay in the car. I'm going to buy us some oranges," he said, getting out of the car. We all watched as he spoke, mostly in gestures, to a stout Quechua woman who wore an apron over her long dark skirt and many underskirts, with a dusty bowler hat perched high on her head.

We left the village with our oranges and slowly made our way up the winding road until we spotted a mountain stream. Dad pulled over and carefully scanned the area ahead and behind us.

"We'll be OK here," he said. "Let's have a drink and fill our thermoses with water from this stream."

"But the missionaries here in Bolivia have all told us that we can't drink the water if it hasn't been boiled," Mom said, her eyes questioningly on my father.

"Not so if the water comes from a mountain stream," Dad said. "It's as pure as it gets. Now hurry up. Get your drinks. We have to keep going."

Mom began filling her thermos with the spring water. I scampered up behind the streambed with my brothers to explore the woods above it. We stopped and abruptly turned when we heard men's shouts approaching us. A dozen or so wild-looking men wearing Basque-style berets and tattered tunics over frayed trousers crowded around the Volvo. They yelled at Dad in Quechua, waving sawed-off shotguns at him.

"*Que quieren*—what do you want?" Dad asked, grabbing Mary Lou and

Nothing Bad Between Us

holding her tight. The men pushed him roughly aside and began to pull out the contents of our car, the food box, Mom's typewriter and two pillows, throwing them to the side of the road.

I stood immobile; every muscle tensed. Warm liquid trickled down the inside of my legs.

Just then, an open Jeep clattered up the hill behind us, two uniformed soldiers in the front seat. The guerillas grabbed an armful of our clothing and ran up the road and off into the brush.

I slipped my wet panties down my legs when no one was looking and threw them behind a bush before climbing back into the car, squished between typewriter-on-her-lap Mom and red-faced David.

"John, I think it's unwise for us to be going to Santa Cruz," Mom said in almost a whisper from the back seat.

"Clara, *bitte hault die*," he growled, revving the car as fast as it would go on the rutted dirt road. "You know that we promised to visit the leprosy colony there. They are expecting our help, and we are going to give it to them."

•••

After Quito, Ecuador, we dropped out of the mountains. The road was flat and sandy. The air blowing in from the open front windows landed hot and heavy on us, like a warm wet blanket. My body was sticky, and my cotton shirt stuck to my skin.

"He pinched me," I yelled, pushing David away from me.

"I did not," he screamed back.

"*Tuppi, tuppi*—potty, potty!" Mary Lou screeched from the back of the car. We all knew what this meant. She had to vomit.

"Stop it, David." This time I pushed him even harder.

Dad stomped on the brakes, sending clouds of dust billowing into the car. "I'm going to load you all onto a plane and send you on," he said, staring back at us, his eyes flaring with anger.

That doesn't seem like a punishment at all, I thought. But I said nothing. We all said nothing. Except our little "songbird" from the back, which is what the folks called Mary Lou. She had perfumed the car with her vomit and now sang, "*Alabaré*, alabaré, alabaré a mi señor—Praise, praise, praise my Lord." Her soft voice floated through the stinky, fuming, dark energy in the car.

"Mary Lou, that's so sweet," Mom said. "And look, here's a perfect place to camp, right next to this waterfall with nice clean water."

That's so sweeeeet, I mouthed in an exaggerated way, turning to frown at my little sister in the back.

• • •

To get from Colombia to Central America, we needed to get through an impassable 280-kilometer (170 mile) stretch of marshland known as the Darién Gap. We boarded a ship in Colombia, the *Amerigo Vespucci*, which took us through the Panama Canal. After eight weeks and about 10,000 kilometers, we left South America and made our way into Central America.

Costa Rica was just finishing its stretch of the Pan-American Highway when we arrived, so the roads were all covered with new gravel and ready for travel.

"*Pero, señor.*" The friendly man at the filling station shook his head. "There are thirty-eight rivers you need to cross. There are not yet bridges across many of those rivers."

"How do people manage to travel on the new road if there aren't bridges?" Dad asked.

"The only vehicles on that road are bulldozers and trucks, all road workers," he said. Seeing the disappointment in Dad's eyes, he continued. "I can get the bridge *ingeniero* [engineer]. He can tell you what you can do."

After a few hours, the *ingeniero* pulled into the gas station in a large yellow diesel truck.

"*Buenos dias,*" he said, shaking Dad's hand.

After hearing that Dad planned to travel across Costa Rica in the Volvo, he shook his head. "We are in the rainy season, *señor*. The rivers are two or three meters (six to eight feet) deep. The only thing you can do is go back to Panama City and take a ship to Nicaragua, skipping Costa Rica entirely."

"But that would mean going two days back to where we came from. That's not an option," Dad said.

The engineer eyed the stubborn man standing in front of him and saw the fire in his dark eyes. "*Señor*, I will drag you through the first river with a bulldozer, but at your own risk. And after that, you are on your own."

"*Gracias.*" Dad shook his hand. There was a bounce in his walk when he approached our car.

"John, is this wise? We don't know how we'll get through the other rivers," Mom said when he announced the plan.

He looked over at her and grinned. "You know, Clara, for me the greatest thrill of this journey will be over once all the questions are answered about how we'll get through what's next."

"Here, I've fixed us a delicious dinner of pineapple and bread and water. Let's eat while we wait for the bulldozer to come," Mom said.

"I'm tired of bread and water. I refuse to eat it," I grumbled.

"That's a good sign that you're not very hungry," Mom said, spreading the slices of pineapple and bread on a tin sheet.

•••

The mud-covered bulldozer slowly made its way to the gas station and the *ingeniero* waved for us to follow it to the first river, just on the outskirts of the town. Its powerful tracks were nearly as high as our Volvo.

"Wow, we're going across *that*? Can we swim across?" My brothers John and Wesley said almost in unison when we reached the riverbank. They jumped out of the car before it came to a full stop.

I shrank back in the seat. The deep currents of dark, churning water scared me. I wished we had gone back.

"Come on, boys. Help get these chains attached to our front bumper. Then we'll hook the chains onto the back of the bulldozer like this." Dad whistled as he hooked our car up to the bulldozer.

I held my breath when we slowly approached the river.

"Dad, we're going to drown!" I cried. Dark, angry waves smashed against the windows. I stared at the worried creases on my father's forehead. But instead of being swallowed beneath the swirling water, our car began to rise. I looked at my folks to see if they thought the Holy Spirit was lifting us. But no. Our Volvo floated. It bobbed up and down. The current dragged us downriver, but the bulldozer steadily kept its course and pulled us to the opposite muddy shore.

After a while, it was no longer breathtakingly scary to cross those rivers. The worst part was waiting for the rafts, the caterpillars, the trucks, or the bulldozers to pull us. We met almost no other vehicles on that road in Costa Rica other than road workers, who all seemed happy to help us.

•••

We crossed the border at El Paso, Texas, one day short of three months from the day we started. The remainder of the journey to Kansas, we drove on the widest, smoothest, straightest highways I had ever seen.

"We did it, Clara." Dad beamed at my mother as we pulled into her folks' driveway in Newton, Kansas. His face broke into a wide grin. Staring at that smile from where I sat in the back seat, I realized that this trip had been the perfect combination of God-work and wild adventure for my father.

I crawled out of the cramped, smelly car, pushing David out of the way. *I will never again, ever, agree to be stuck in a car for that long*, I promised myself. *No matter what.*

•••

Shortly after the trip, I began to lose a lot of weight, had constant diarrhea with blood, and ran a high fever. My folks took me to medical specialists in the States, who poked and prodded and took specimens of every kind of bodily fluid. It took months before the American doctors finally discovered that I had amoebae living in my intestines. Amoebae are uncommon in the States, since they are parasites found mostly in developing countries. They enter the body through the mouth when one ingests food or drink contaminated with feces that contain somebody's excreted parasites. I was the only one who picked up the parasite on our trip.

A clipping of my parents being interviewed in 1960 for a Kansas newspaper article, published just a few months before my amoebic symptoms began, reads, "Surprisingly, none of the children became ill. The Schmidts were extremely wary of local food supplies because of the prevalence of amoebic dysentery."

•••

After some months in the US raising money and prayers for the leprosy work, we flew back home to Paraguay, leaving my oldest three siblings in the States with relatives to continue their education. The following year, my brother David and I were sent to the big city of Asunción to go to school. We got to come home to Km. 81 on weekends and during the summer vacation months.

CHAPTER 3:
A Child's Be-Longing (1961–1963)

Our family in 1960—I'm in front on the left

———

"Some of us aren't meant to belong. Some of us have to turn the world upside down and shake the hell out of it until we make our own place in it."

—Elizabeth Lowell, *Remember Summer*

———

I was at home at the leprosy station for summer vacation. It was an early January evening, the air still heavy with the day's steamy heat. Our family sat around the blue laminate-topped table on our veranda, finishing our supper of warm boiled rice with sugar and cinnamon. I started to clear the table and said to my father, "I'm not going to the meeting tonight." The meeting we kids were required to attend every Wednesday evening lasted for two never-ending hours of boring prayers that droned on and on.

"You are going," he said.

"No, I'm not. You can't make me." I stomped away from the table.

"Come back here," he yelled.

I continued toward the girls' room and slammed the door as hard as I could.

That's when he came after me.

"I don't know why you always make me do this." Dad's voice was thick with anger. He grabbed my arm and pulled me along behind him, out of the girls' bedroom, out to the veranda that surrounded our house, and toward his room. Even though I knew I couldn't win, I tugged back with all of my weight and dug my heels hard against the uneven tiles of the veranda. But my nine-year-old body was no match for my father's strong, six-foot frame. With his free hand, he turned the round wooden doorknob to his room and shoved me through the door. Without making a sound, I coiled my body away from him like a crazed wild animal.

Roughly pulling me along, he snatched the leather strap from the hook in his bedroom and wet it in the corner water basin. I kicked and writhed to get out of his grip, but this only made him grasp me more fiercely. His left hand dug into my skull and grabbed a handful of my thick hair, as he pushed my head down between the bed and his thigh, pinning me under his leg. While one arm held my thrashing body down against his leg, he pushed his other hand up under my skirt and yanked down my cotton panties.

"No, no, Daddy, no," I howled into the coarse bedspread. But the strap came down hard. Once. Twice. Three times. Four. Five.

By the time he pushed me aside and stood to leave, I'd stopped screaming.

"Tell me you're sorry." He glared at me, eyes fiery with rage. I glowered back, saying nothing, panties dangling around my ankles.

"Then sit here and think about it and come out when you are ready to say you are sorry," he growled, walking out and slamming the door behind him.

With angry tears still stinging my eyes, I knelt on the floor and twisted around to inspect my scorching buttocks. I knew what I would find there. I'd seen it many times before. Rows of welts were already beginning to form where each blow had struck me, and blood oozed from them, creating a maze of red trails across my backside.

Gingerly, I pulled up my homemade panties, the rough cotton scuffing against the gashes. "I will never, ever tell him I'm sorry," I muttered to myself, still on my knees.

After what seemed like hours, I heard the wooden doorknob click and sensed rather than saw him moving toward me. I knelt by the bed, my eyes closed to keep from looking at him. But I held my head high and my chin thrust out defiantly.

"Tell me you're sorry," he hissed. My body recoiled from the fury still in his voice, and I knew it wasn't over. I said nothing.

"You give me no choice," he said through clenched teeth, and turned to wet the strap again.

•••

He who withholds his rod hates his son, but he who loves him disciplines him diligently, says the Bible. Despite loathing all the long prayer meetings and tedious sermons, I was Mennonite enough to know that I was sinful, fallen, and constantly in need of reform and repair. I knew how much my father loved me. That's why he punished me so diligently.

I knew that and accepted it, and I also rebelled against it.

As far back as I can remember, there was that sort of paradoxical tension between my dad and me. On one hand, I longed to be close to him and to emulate him, and on the other, I defied him and wanted to not be at all like him. I understood my father and his leprosy work and the whole Mennonite tribe to be so right, so correct, and so respected in the world that I desperately wanted to be a part of it. At the same time, I felt a powerful hostility toward Dad and all the righteousness that I thought he represented.

The tension between us apparently preceded my birth. My father had "special-ordered" me. I knew the story well. I was supposed to be born on April 18. My mother wanted me to appear on the 19th, her father's birthday. "It's such a big baby, I'm sure it's a boy, and we'll name him Bernie after my dad," she announced to my father a few days before my due date. "I want us to induce labor if the baby isn't here by the 19th so that he's born on my dad's birthday."

My father had no patience for such nonsense. "No such thing. Quinine and castor oil are poisons that may stimulate early labor, but you might as well be back with ignorant midwives if you go that route." Dad thought midwives were part of the dark ages, so this was quite a forceful statement. "Besides," he told her, "it's not a boy. It's a dark-haired, dark-eyed girl, just like I ordered."

Despite his protestations, my mother insisted, and on the afternoon of April 18 she checked into the hospital. The doctor carefully separated the membranes from Mom's cervix and inserted repeated doses of castor oil and quinine, waiting twenty minutes between doses. Her body reacted violently to the poisons, leading to the inevitable diarrhea and uterine contractions, but stubbornly, I didn't budge. Finally, even my mother gave up the mission and they went home.

On the 23rd, I made my move. Dad helped Mom walk the hospital halls for a while during the evening and then put her to bed to rest between contractions. She dozed off but awakened in a panic early the next morning when her water broke and contractions were close together, every one to three minutes.

Minutes later my father caught me in his bare hands. "A girl with dark hair and dark eyes," he announced, "just like I ordered."

"And stubborn, just like you, John," my mom would often say.

•••

I directed my obstinacy beyond my father to his tribe, the Mennonite church. I was never sure about the whole Jesus-died-to-save-me part even though I felt guilty about questioning it. Mostly, I hated how everything that seemed like it would be fun was a sin. Like listening to lively music or daydreaming or wearing makeup or shaving my legs. Sometimes I wasn't even sure why something was a sin, like the V-shaped blouse I wanted to sew for myself. Mom told me that this was forbidden because the "V" line pointed down to my vaginal area and it would surely present a temptation for boys. At the age of nine, I didn't really know what she was talking about. But because it was forbidden, I wanted it even more.

My rebelliousness meant that Dad spanked me harder and more often than all of his other kids combined. I recently asked my older sister to describe to me the kinds of things I did that would cause him to strike me so often and so hard. "You were the defiant one," she said. "From what I remember, you were the only one of Dad's children who openly challenged him. Even when you were tiny, if he drew a line in the sand, you looked him in the eye and put your foot over it."

When the beatings were over, I used to show off my bloody backside to my siblings. A part of me believed that my dad hated me. But the other part believed that because he beat me the most, he must love me the most.

"Look at this," I said to my brother David, who stood just outside of our parents' room, probably listening in on my torment. I pulled down my panties and bent over so he could see the bloody stripes.

"You think that makes you so special, don't you?" he sneered, sticking his tongue out at me.

•••

Other than morning prayers with all of us together, our parents were hardly ever home. Dad prayed long, arduous prayers for global peace, for the wisdom of the world's political leaders, for the health of each extended family member, and for the well-being of those less fortunate than we. His prayers went on and on. And then my parents would leave for the day. I was never sure exactly what they were doing, but I knew it was important work for the Lord. A woman named Aggie looked after us, but she didn't look or act anything like a mom. She almost always had a stern face and a heavy hand. But she was as wide as she was tall, so we didn't dare mess with her.

One day I overheard Aggie talking to my mother. "Marlena sits in her room a lot, brooding. There are no kids her age here on the station, so she spends an awful lot of time alone. She seems very cross most of the time, too. You know I'm busy taking care of all of the laundry, the cleaning and the cooking. And there's little Mary Lou to watch. I just don't have time for that angry girl of yours. I don't know what to do with her."

Mom spotted me standing near them and called out, "Marlena, come here. What seems to be the problem?"

I wanted to say, "I hate it here. I don't have anyone to play with. I feel like I'm in a prison with no way to ever get out. And I don't know why this God-work is so important to you." What I said out loud was, "The problem? What problem? Aggie always says everything I do is a problem." And I stomped off to sulk in the girls' room.

···

I was twelve when Cresencio came into our home.

The day he arrived, I was in a particularly dark mood. It was only the first week of summer vacation, and I had already fallen into my normal pattern at home. Bored, sullen, and moody, I was sulking in my room when I heard Mom's voice.

"Marlena, look what we have here. This is Cresencio. He's two."

In her arms was an emaciated child whose head looked way too big for his tiny frail arms and legs. A large swollen belly protruded from the tattered rags he wore. I looked into the warmest big brown eyes I had ever seen.

"What's wrong with him? Why is his tummy so huge?" I asked, reaching over to touch his skinny brown arms.

"There's a lot wrong," Mom said. "His tummy is full of worms and he's almost starved to death, but the worst part is that he has tuberculosis. Bad. He's going to stay with us for a while so we can nurse him back to health."

"Can I hold him?" I asked, feeling a surge of compassion for this helpless sick child with big chocolate eyes.

Ever so gently I took him from my mother's arms and placed him on a chair so I could take the dirty rags off his back. My arms reached out to steady him when I saw that he couldn't sit on his own.

Up until this moment, Cresencio hadn't made a sound. Now he looked up at me and let out a feeble cry. "Ga, ga."

It was the closest I had ever felt to someone else. Until she went to live in the States to continue her schooling there, my older sister had looked after my little sister Mary Lou like a mother, leaving me feeling sidelined. Now I was needed and loved. For the rest of the summer, I rarely left Cresencio's side. I pulled long tapeworms from his butt, taught him how to sit and then walk, and played endless games with a ball he loved. Even my folks called him "Marlena's Chrissy." By the end of my summer vacation, he was a happy toddler with fat cheeks, and I had just had the best summer of my life.

It was early March, the air still heavy and humid. I was cooling Cresencio down by squirting him from a bucket of water.

Mom came out of the house toward us and said the dreaded words.

"Marlena, he's healthy now and his lungs are clear. It's time for us to take him back to his mother."

As though knowing what those words meant, or maybe sensing my distress, Cresencio tottered toward me and clasped both arms around my leg.

"We can't do... How can we do that... Can't we keep him...?" The words fell out of my mouth in a jumble.

"I've already gathered his clothes and toys. Daddy will take us to where his mom lives." She pulled my boy away from me.

I crawled into the back of our brown station wagon and clasped Cresencio in my lap. How could they take away from me the one person who loved me so completely? The one person who needed me? And how could they even consider abandoning him now that he felt safe with us? The boy wrapped his arms around my neck like he knew that something terrible was about to happen.

Dad parked in front of the hut. On the hard-packed dirt floor of the open shack stood a stooped woman with a baby in her arms and three older children hanging onto her skirt, suspiciously eyeing the big car that had pulled into their yard. The place smelled of wood smoke from the smoldering coals in the middle of the floor.

Dad jumped out of the car, opened the back door, and pulled Cresencio out of my arms. "It's time to let him go, Marlena," he said gruffly.

I threw my body out of the car and tried to grab him out of my father's grip. "No Daddy, please...no...no...we can't leave him in this dump," I screamed. The woman and her children backed up, their eyes large with fear.

Dad walked briskly toward the woman and began to hand her son over to her. I felt sick and ran behind the car to vomit. With acid still stinging in my throat, I made my way back around to the front of the vehicle. Dad and the woman were having an animated conversation I couldn't understand because I spoke little Spanish. But when he turned back toward us, Cresencio still in his arms, the heavy weight on my chest began to lift.

"She doesn't want him back. She says her hands are full with the children she has. She says she can't feed them all and she also wants us to take in Cresencio's younger sister Josefina," he said, looking at me darkly as though it was all my fault.

•••

When I got into trouble and Dad was angry with me, I knew I could always hide out in the safety of my own private sanctuary in the woods. Our family house at the station was a red brick L-shaped structure, with a veranda running all the way along the two sides of the L. It was set back in the woods a bit, maybe a hundred meters from the other houses on the station. To get from our house to the other cluster of houses, we had to walk through a dense forest of *Cedro, Lapacho, Ibyraró,* and *Palo Rosa.*

I spent many hours in that forest. I ripped out a path with a machete as deeply as I could into the woods, and at the end of that path, I cleared an area for my own little home. Pieces of lumber crudely hammered together became my table and chairs. Old rice sacks neatly lined up on the ground served as my bed. In the center of my kitchen, I built a stove by placing several old bricks on top of one another to surround a small area that would hold the fire. With some twigs and matches, there it was, a reliable stove.

When I was finished, I had a fine home. Our family's house was often cluttered and dusty. Everything in my forest home was always neat and orderly. Precise circles of stones around the perimeter marked my walls. Within them, I felt safe. I lay on my rice-sack bed or sat on my makeshift chairs and tried to come up with more and better home improvements.

For meals, I stole vegetables from the main gardens of the leprosy station. Carrots mostly, since they grew in a relatively hidden area of the garden where no one could see me pull them out of the warm earth. And parsley too, which was planted in the beds right next to the carrots.

Here's the recipe for one of the most common meals in my forest home:

- 3 carrots, greens pulled off, broken into pieces
- 1 small handful of parsley
- Pour water into an old tin can dug out of a garbage pit
- Light a fire in the stove, and place the can of water directly on the fire
- Once the water boils, place the broken pieces of carrot and the parsley in the water
- Cook until tender.

Nothing Bad Between Us

To this day, like Proust and his *madeleines*, when I smell parsley and carrots cooking, I am taken back to my first home and the domestic pleasures of cleaning and cooking in my own little space.

I also had a toilet. I cleared a little area directly behind my kitchen and dug a hole in the center of it with a spade I borrowed from the leprosy station's tool shed. I worried that my father would find out about my toilet. Believing that hygiene has a lot to do with contracting leprosy, one of his main missions was to teach people not to pee or poop near their food and water supply. There was little chance he'd discover my hiding place, though, absent as he was from my life. So I was safe in my own little home.

•••

Despite the raging tensions between Dad and me, I could always get his attention when I needed medical care.

Like the night I woke up when I was twelve with a sharp pain in my chest. I didn't know what a heart attack felt like, but I was sure I was having one. So I banged on my folks' bedroom door, opened it just a crack, and whispered, "Daddy, I'm having a heart attack."

"Describe to me exactly where the pain is," he said calmly, pulling on a pair of pants. I pointed to my chest, covered in a loose nightshirt. Without warning, he gave my chest a sharp slap and the trapped air bubble escaped. No more heart attack! I went back to my room and fell promptly back to sleep. I felt lucky to have a dad who could save me when I might have died.

And then there were the pinworms. Pinworms were rampant among all of us kids. We passed them around, I suppose, by not washing our hands after going to the outhouse toilet. My pinworm problems were worst at night when the female worms were most active and crawled out of the anus to deposit their eggs.

We also had hookworms quite often, caused by walking barefooted on ground contaminated with fecal matter. All of us kids at the leprosy station ran around barefooted. My folks considered shoes to be frivolous and unnecessary for us kids, except for church on Sundays. Hookworm larvae can penetrate the skin of the foot, and once inside the body, they migrate to the lungs and from there up the trachea and are swallowed. They then pass down the esophagus and enter the digestive system, finishing their journey in the intestine, where the larvae mature into adult worms. This can become life threatening.

Whenever my feet got too itchy, I would run over to the clinic to show them to Dad. "Look, I have blisters on my feet again," I said.

"Come let me take a look." I loved how concerned my father always became when I came to him with blisters on my feet.

He disappeared into his little pharmacy area at the back of the clinic and returned with a little vial of colorless liquid. "Drink this," he ordered. I smelled the familiar sweet odor and frowned, knowing how icky it would taste. But I drank it as instructed.

I understood the importance of killing off the larvae by drinking this awful concoction, which I now know was tetrachloroethylene, a Group 2A carcinogen. It is a nonflammable solvent widely used today as a dry-cleaning agent and degreaser in the automotive and other metalworking industries, as well as a paint stripper and spot remover. The carcinogen may have harmed us, but at the time, it was all there was to treat hookworm infestation. My father could cure anything, even if it hurt us.

•••

I always thought my father was larger than life. Sometimes I even knew that he was, like one night when I heard a rap on my bedroom door. "Marlena, your mother and I need your help with a patient. Now."

Still half asleep, I stumbled over to the clinic. My eyes fell on the bloody mass of a child's face and head. It was a little girl, maybe seven years old. She'd caught her long braids in the chute that directs corn down to a horse-drawn corn grinder. The grinder had literally ripped the skin above her eyes and had pulled her scalp loose from her head. The tear stretched all the way across her face. Her eyeballs hung down onto her cheeks. It took her family six hours in an ox-drawn cart to get to Dad's clinic. The child was near death when they arrived.

My mother was lighting a kerosene lamp and Dad was carrying the girl to the examining table when I entered the clinic. The child's parents stood quietly over to the side, as my father barked orders in staccato to my mother and me. "Quick. Over here. Hold this lamp, Marlena. Clara, give me those clamps. I need the alcohol."

That night I held the kerosene lamp and watched with awe and repulsion as my father stitched the tattered scalp back together, carefully lining it up with the child's eyes.

Years later I saw a photo of her that her family had sent to my dad. A faint scar across her face at eye level was the only blemish on the beaming face of that young girl.

•••

Paradoxical tensions raged in my belly during those early years at the leprosy station. Between knowing my father was a hero and at the same time loathing his brutality. Between knowing I was bad and deserving of his punishment while also railing against it. Between knowing that the leprosy work, God's work, was all-important and wishing someone would destroy it.

Dad continued to beat me into my preteen years. At over five feet tall and 120 pounds, I was almost grown. But his strength still easily overpowered me, and there I was again, screaming in terror, my head pinned under his left thigh. This time, when he yanked my panties down, a mass of bloody rags fell into his hands. We had no maxi pads or tampons in Paraguay in those days. Our menstrual blood collected in large rags that we changed and washed out by hand.

His hands dropped to his side. He released my head and legs. Without a word, he left the room.

CHAPTER 4:
Magical Holidays (1961)

Baking Christmas Pfeffernuesse

*"The holidays drape us in magic and
give us the hope that we can do better
than we have done in the past."*

—Toni Sorenson

One Easter morning at around four o'clock, Dad woke us up with his usual loud "rise and shine" as he passed by on the veranda outside our bedrooms. It was early April with cool fall nights. We had no heaters, so getting out from under the covers should have been hard. But on this morning, we scrambled out and were ready to go in minutes.

It was time to climb the *Osterberg* (Easter Hill) to watch the sun rise, like we did every year. It was the most fun part about Easter.

"Here's a flashlight," Dad said. "Watch your little sister." I was ten. Mary Lou was four. My little Cresencio and his sister Josefina had not yet joined our family.

We made our way the short distance through the forest to the *Andere Haus* (other house), which is what we called the central kitchen and dining hall. The station workers were already assembled. The women were wrapped in dark shawls; the men wore ponchos or jackets. Together we walked the two and a half kilometers (about a mile and a half) to the *Ruta* (highway), mostly in silence. The only sound was a soft murmuring among some of the women up ahead. There must have been forty or fifty of us in that procession in the chilly darkness of the autumn pre-dawn. The dew evaporating in the morning air brought out the thick musty smells of the clay-rich soil.

Before long, I fell back behind the rest, leaving Mary Lou to fend for herself. I turned off my flashlight. Standing still, I stared up at the night sky still shimmering with stars that surrounded me like an immense canopy stretching from one horizon to the other.

I had suffered through the church services on Good Friday. I had endured the sermons and long prayers about Jesus's death on the cross. I loved the hymn singing part. I just didn't understand why people thought their sins were forgiven because some man died on a cross almost two thousand years ago. But here on this dirt road off by myself, enveloped in the starlight, I felt a profound awe, even reverence. I tilted my face up to the sky and a slight shudder ran through me. *Is this what it feels like to be in God's presence?* I wondered. I didn't know what to make of this, and I never spoke of it to anyone.

I rushed to catch up with the rest and found my little sister. Just across the *Ruta* was the hill we called the *Osterberg*. There it was. It looked immense. We crossed the *Ruta* and walked the short distance to the foot of the hill. Little shudders ran up and down my spine.

The group splintered, each person searching for a way through the thick brush on the hill. I clutched the flashlight in one hand and pulled Mary Lou along with the other, eyes down, searching for snakes. I knew they hung out in this brush since we had more than once encountered a rattlesnake on this hill. I was terrified of snakes.

"Don't step there. A snake'll get you for sure," I said, transferring my fear to my little sister. She started to cry. I shook her to try to get her to stop. I always got into trouble when she cried about something I did. But the more I shook her, the more she cried.

"*Wot ess dit*? Why can't you just behave yourself?" Dad came up from behind us and pulled Mary Lou up onto his shoulders, giving me one of his

Nothing Bad Between Us

stern looks.

As I watched him stride ahead of me, I shrank back into the brush. I knew I needed to behave myself, especially when we were with the station volunteers. We kids had been told a million times that they were God's Helpers and we needed to be respectful and well-behaved around them. "I'm sorry," I whispered to no one under my breath.

Once we reached the top of the hill, the first rays of the sun painted a red glow across the eastern horizon. We all broke into singing my favorite Easter hymns. Then the long sermon and prayers started, and my mind began to wander as it always did.

I daydreamed about the fudge. At Easter, Mom would make lots of fudge of different varieties. Mom didn't really cook much when we were young. Aggie, the woman who raised us, or other Helpers would normally cook for us. But around the holidays, Mom spent days in the kitchen, mostly making fudge. The pink fudge was almond flavored. The green was mint flavored. And of course, the brown chocolate fudge was the very best.

I thought about how we had spent hours decorating all those hard-boiled eggs. Given that we were painting eggs for all of the patients and the station workers, we had to buy extra eggs from the neighboring town. Our chickens couldn't keep up. A few days prior, we had gathered with all of the station workers at the *Andere Haus*. At the end of the evening, we had adorned several large buckets full of eggs.

We had also made Easter baskets by gluing together pieces of colorful construction paper and stapling paper strips over the top for the handles. Many dozens of them, enough for all of the leprosy patients who lived on the station, for God's Helpers and their families, and for our own family. I daydreamed about those baskets filled with fudge and colorful eggs, which would be hidden in places all over the station. I never knew exactly how they got there.

"Denn dein ist das Reich und die Kraft und die Herrlichkeit in Ewigkeit. Amen." The last "Amen" shook me from my reverie. The sun was fully up. We ran down the hill, the other kids and I ahead of the rest of them, snakes and God-presence forgotten, excited to get home to the station for the Easter basket hunt.

•••

Christmas was the best holiday of all. It was when our family seemed like a normal family. A family like other people had.

Every year MCC (Mennonite Central Committee) collected donations from Mennonites back in the States and shipped barrels full of wonderful stuff to us and to other missionaries around the world to hand out to our patients and to other poor people at Christmastime. We kids even got some things.

The MCC barrels had arrived. They stood sealed and silent as though taunting me when I periodically peeked into the warehouse where they were lined up. I was dying to know what was in them this year.

Finally, it was time to open them. A number of women at the station had constructed three long tables in the warehouse with planks of wood supported by sawhorses at the ends of each one. We stood in a semicircle, about ten of us, including my mother and me and the station workers, as one of them pried open the mysterious containers from the north.

The lids fell open. I breathed in deeply, savoring that sweet fragrance I could always count on. At the time, it would have been hard for me to describe that "United States smell." Today I know it as the distinctive new-clothes smell of US department stores.

I hopped from one foot to the other. "Can I see what's in this one?"

"Settle down, Marlena," my mother said. "We can't get into the other barrels until we've emptied this one with the towels." She lifted out one large, soft, fluffy bath towel after another and handed them to us. I knew the drill. We used the towels as wrapping for other items we would place inside them, and then we'd pin each one up into a neat package.

I put each luxurious towel against my face and deeply breathed in the magical perfume before passing it along the assembly line we had formed. We folded them and then carefully placed them in rows along the makeshift tables.

Finally, Mom began to hand us items from the other barrels. Washcloths, soap, combs, bottles of shampoo and shaving cream, as well as small items of clothing and children's toys.

"Oh, smell this soap," I held the bar up to Marichen, a heavyset woman working beside me, her long braids wrapped like yellow garlands around her head. "It smells like flowers. If I get some soap like this in my towel, I won't ever use it. I'll just keep it right next to my bed where I can always smell it," I added wistfully.

Along with other station workers, I stood at the long tables and sorted the new things into separate piles. "Now remember," my mother said, watching me hug item after item to my chest. It felt like the best candy store. "Remember, put only one toiletry item, one washcloth, and one piece of clothing into each towel. We need to make almost a hundred towel packages this year."

The towel packages went into big boxes marked "Women," "Men," "Boys," and "Girls." We made packages for the leprosy patients, for neighboring Paraguayan families, and for station volunteer workers and their families.

"Now you need to leave," Mom said, looking at me with a smile.

I knew what that meant. She was going to make a towel package for us kids. "Please, please, Mom, can I pleeeeecccase help you make David's and Mary Lou's? I promise to leave when you make mine."

"Run along," Mom said. "I want their towel packages to be a surprise for you too."

•••

I could smell the cinnamon and cloves and anise seed out on the veranda even before entering the kitchen. As I came in, I saw Mom standing over a large bowl, kneading a doughy mass, one side of her face spattered with flour.

I grinned, pinched off a bit of the dough between two fingers, and popped it into my mouth. "Can we start now?"

"Go get your brother and sister," she said. "I think we're ready."

"Time for *Pfeffer*nüsse," I yelled out the open door, rather than getting them. I couldn't wait to get my hands into the dough.

*Pfeffer*nüsse, which translates to peppernuts, are popular Christmas treats in Germany, Denmark, and the Netherlands, as well as among Mennonites in North and South America. They are tiny spice cookies about the size and shape of hazelnuts. We were always excited about making them together as a family, although I don't remember my father ever being a part of this activity.

"Can I please start rolling the dough?" I asked.

My brother David and little Mary Lou came through the door just as I finished rolling a portion of dough into a long, thin snake.

"Hey, no fair starting without us," David said, grabbing the end of my snake and snapping it around until it broke into pieces.

"Mom, tell David to stop. He ruined my snake." I pushed my brother aside.

"Stop fighting, children. Here's your portion, David," Mom said, handing him a big glob. "Louie, come here and we'll work on making a snaky together."

We rolled out our snakes, cut them into small pieces, ate lots of the pieces, and then put what was left of them on cookie sheets to bake.

The aroma of our freshly baked *Pfeffernüsse* wafted out of the kitchen windows and door. Now it smelled like Christmas at our house.

•••

Finally, it was the week before Christmas.

"It's time to get our tree up," Dad announced after his long morning prayer. Every Christmas season, he took a whole morning off from his devotion to God's work to help us put up the tree.

I squealed and jumped from my chair. "Can I help you cut down the branches?"

"*Najo* [roughly translated from Low German, this means "OK" or "well"]. Come with me. You can choose which branches we should cut."

Saw in hand, my father led the way into the fields, where small scrappy-looking pine trees were just starting to mature. He had explained to me many times that it was wrong to ever cut down any of those trees. But we could carefully trim off some of the branches. "That way the tree can continue to live," he said.

We came back from the fields, our arms full of pine branches of various lengths. Dad had drilled holes at an angle all the way up and down a wooden sawed-off broomstick. The pole, attached to a platform of cross boards, stood about five feet tall. "Would you like to decide which branches are just the right length and start sticking them into the holes in the pole?" I thought maybe his eyes were smiling at me, and my heart did a little happy dance.

"Let's do it together, you and me, Daddy," I said.

When we were done, our branches, inserted into each of the holes, more or less formed the shape of a single five-foot Christmas tree. Dad and I stood back, pleased with our work.

"Beautiful," Mom said, coming out to the veranda where the tree stood. "Now let's make some garlands." She placed a large bowl of popped corn on the table. "Where are the others?"

While she rounded up my brother and sister, I started by threading a needle, and then, slowly and carefully so the corn wouldn't split in half, pushed the needle through one piece of popped corn at a time.

"Mary Lou, can you hold the end up while I keep sliding more corn along the thread?" I asked. My little sister held on to the end and patiently waited until we had made a really long white strand.

"*Schön, schön*—pretty, pretty," she said in her childish German, clapping her hands together.

Mom started clipping little candleholders onto the tree's branches. We didn't have clip-holders to fasten the candles to the branches, like the kind you can purchase online today. But we made our own clip-holders with wire that we had gotten from the station workshop. We snipped the wire into short segments and then wrapped them around the candle base and the tree branch.

"Mom, please, I know it's not dark yet, but can I please, please light the candles? Just for a minute?" I was skipping around and around our tree, nearly bursting with the excitement of it all. I thought we had the most beautiful and magical tree ever.

As I lit the candles, I heard my mother behind me, humming my favorite German Christmas carol, "*O du fröhliche, o du selige, gnadenbringende Weihnachtszeit!*" (Roughly translated: "Oh you joyful, oh you blessed, merciful Christmastime.") I felt a great big wave of warmth spread through my chest. This was exactly the way I wanted family to feel all the time. Only it didn't.

...

Christmas Eve was a hot summer night. It was almost seven o'clock, but the sun was still blazing in the western sky. I heard the cicadas continue to sing all around me, competing with the chatter of the frogs and crickets.

I was alone on our veranda, pacing back and forth. *What was taking them so long?* I wondered. We had taken our weekly shower and were dressed in our Sunday best. I wore a brand-new red dress my mother had sewn for me.

"Let's all walk over together," Mom said, straightening out the big, light-blue bow in Mary Lou's curly blond hair.

The station workers and our family began the evening by serenading all of the leprosy patients and bringing them towel packages and plates heaped high with Mom's fudge, a popcorn ball, and often an apple. When we arrived, the patients had already gathered around in a circle in an open courtyard. Some of them lay on the ground or squatted and others stood when we arrived, offering us their stools or chairs. They weren't dressed any differently, I noticed. They didn't have any Sunday best.

Someone had already piled all of the towel packages on a nearby table. I helped carry one to each patient. "*Feliz Navidad,*" I said, as I delivered each one. *Doña Ramona*'s face beamed as I helped her open the towel and placed the items against her face so she could sense the beauty.

"*Feliz Navidad. Muchas gracias. Feliz Navidad.*" The air around us vibrated with joy, as the toothless, limbless, blind, and crippled people in that circle showered their love on us.

We all held hands and together sang a few verses of "*Noche de Paz, Noche de Amor*" ("Silent Night, Holy Night").

Then the really fun part started. I skipped all the way from the circle of leprosy patients to the *Andere Haus*, the main meetinghouse on the station. Long tables draped in white cloths had been set up in the yard, laden with towel packages and treats. All of the station personnel, as well as Paraguayan families from the surrounding area, had already gathered around the tables and were curiously eyeing the treasures.

But I knew that first there would be lots of singing and then those long, tedious prayers to get through. As the prayers droned on, I daydreamed about

Nothing Bad Between Us

what might be in my towel package. I hoped I would get one of those sweet-smelling bars of soap.

Finally. My fingers shook as I undid the safety pins on my package. There it was. Wrapped in pink, with the words *LUX Beauty-Soap* across it and a picture of a pretty lady's face. I held it in both hands and looked up. My mother was watching me, smiling.

•••

Early Christmas morning, before the ten o'clock service with the leprosy patients, was all ours. Just our family, like it almost never was at any other time. I had barely slept the night before. I placed the precious items from my towel package neatly beside my bed and periodically reached over to bring the soft washcloth or the fragrant soap up against my face. Over and over I imagined the magic the next morning would bring.

We kids sprang out of bed early and lined up outside the living room door on our veranda, from the youngest closest to the door, to the oldest (still at home) farthest away. We stood and waited. I could hardly stand still. Finally, we heard Mom starting to play "*Stille Nacht, Heilige Nacht*" ("Silent Night, Holy Night") on her portable pump organ in the living room.

"OK, we're ready for you. *Jie tjenne nü nenn kohme*—you can come in now," Dad called out. On tiptoes, Mary Lou turned the round wooden doorknob and we marched in. There it was, the big blue-topped dining room table that usually stood on our veranda, in the center of our living room. Around the table, the folks had placed large plates, one for each of us, laden with candy, *Pfeffer*nüsse, nuts, and an apple. Apples were a big deal because they didn't grow in Paraguay, so they were imported, usually from Argentina. We each located our plates around the table and waited while Mom and Dad finished singing the carol. I spotted the beautiful pen placed next to my apple, the exact pen I had wished for. Dad stood beside the organ and led the melody with his soaring tenor voice. Mom pumped vigorously on the organ while harmonizing with her alto voice.

As I think about those Christmas mornings, remembering us kids lining up outside the living room door, I realize that my excitement had less to do with the *Pfeffernüsse*, apple, or even the candies or gift I was about to receive. What I loved most was the sound of our parents singing that Christmas carol just for us. And the image of that scene most clearly etched in my memory is the radiant look on their faces when they watched us file into the living room.

In that moment, I felt loved. I felt special. I wished that were how it felt all the time.

CHAPTER 5:
Asunción (1961–1966)

Me at the Km. 81 entrance catching a bus to Asunción

———

*"There is a sense of danger in leaving what you
know, even if what you know isn't much."*

—John William Tuohy

———

For the first few years that I went to school in Asunción when I was ten and
eleven, I lived with other missionary families who were the instruments for
this round of "God will provide." Because they supported my parents' great
work for the Lord, it seemed they had no choice but to take me in. The first
family was the worst. The Wiens must have been really good Christians,
devoutly believing the "God will provide" motto, because they agreed to keep
both my brother David and me in Asunción during the 1961–1962 school
year. The Wiens had four children of their own. Peter Wiens, the dad, was
never at home, busy as he was with important MCC business, just like my
parents. We were told to behave ourselves because Claire, the mom, had
"nerve problems." She spent a lot of time screaming at us and slamming
the doors.

The Wiens's place was what Americans would call an apartment, with
tile floors, high ceilings, and big heavy wooden doors. The two windowless

bedrooms that housed all six of us kids were adjoining rooms so narrow they could barely fit the two clunky wooden bunk beds in each room. To exit the girls' room, we had to go through the boys' room and then through a small bathroom and out into the hall.

On a humid Friday afternoon in October, I lay on the top bunk of the bed that they had assigned to me, drenched in sweat. My mattress was hot and sticky, and the stale air around me felt oppressive.

I was sick. The flu? I no longer remember, but I knew it was a serious inconvenience for the Wiens, who didn't have time to babysit a kid who was just generally a pain to have around to begin with. *If I was just a nicer person, someone the Wiens could like, this wouldn't be happening,* I thought. And from there, my tortured ten-year-old mind wandered off to the many things I had done to not be likable. Like when I teased their five-year-old and hid her doll. Like when I tattled on my brother, telling the Wiens that he hadn't brushed his teeth in a week. Like when I left the supper table and ran out into their backyard instead of helping clear the table.

I turned the hard roll that served as my pillow around so the moisture from my sweat wouldn't stick to my neck and my already matted hair. The other side hadn't dried out from the last time I turned it, so I threw it over the side and rested my head on the hard board that was my bed, covered only by a thin cotton pad and a rough sheet.

I could trace the searing pain from my forehead, down the right side of my head and into my neck. *If this turns into a migraine,* I groaned miserably to myself, *I'm in big trouble, because I'm not sure I can even get down off this bed when I have to vomit.* I knew all about migraines. My father had them regularly and I had just begun getting migraines that year. For both my father and me, migraines always progressed predictably from a severe headache to vomiting.

I missed my dad. He would know what to do to ease this pain. How could I even get someone to help me get down from this bed and to the bathroom? I could hear the maid in the kitchen, pans clattering. She couldn't hear me. The other kids were in school, and Claire seemed to be out. I was alone.

When I woke up, the room was dark. Someone had turned off the little light on the nightstand. I could hear the sounds of suppertime chatter coming from the kitchen. The smell of fried meat was nauseating. I must have slept for hours. I needed to pee, and my head was still throbbing, but it didn't seem to be a migraine. "Can someone help me get down out of this bed?" I called as loudly as I could muster. Nothing. I tried again. "Pleeeeease, can someone help me?"

Claire came to the door and switched on the light. "What's the problem?" Her voice was harsh with annoyance that I was disturbing her supper.

"Can you help me get down and go to the bathroom? My head feels dizzy." With a sigh, she offered her hand.

"Did you wet the bed?" she exclaimed with disgust as her hand touched my wet mattress.

My sweat had soaked through the thin mat. I remembered how upset Mom used to be when I was younger and wet my bed. "It's not pee, really it's not."

I don't think she believed me, judging by the rough way she guided me into the bathroom, slamming the door behind her. A few minutes later she reappeared and helped me back up into my sweat-drenched bed. "Your father was here this afternoon, checking in on you," she said.

"Really? Daddy was here?" Tears stung my eyes. They must have called him. My father cared enough about me that he had stopped in to see me while in town for his regular Friday Asunción shopping day for leprosy station supplies.

"What did he say? Did he come into the room to see me?" I asked.

"I have no idea," she said. "The maid told me that he came by."

When she left the room, I buried my face into the soaked mat and cried. I felt sick and tired and awful, yes, but these were happy tears. I choked into my mat, "Daddy, you were here. You checked in on me while you were in town."

The next day I learned that Dad had brought me a Fanta and that David drank it when he got home from school. He said he didn't know it was supposed to be for me.

•••

Dad often came into Asunción on Fridays to do his weekly shopping for the station. Sometimes, if there was room in the car, I could get a ride home for the weekend. Grain for the livestock, machinery for the metal workers, big bags of rice—those were the sorts of items that would load down the station wagon.

We had a specified meeting place, usually around the *Pettirossi* outdoor marketplace, which was on his way out of town. Dad was almost always late. He was always frazzled. Sometimes he had a migraine headache.

"I've waited on this corner for almost two hours. It's dark and it's late," I complained grumpily, one rainy, cold winter Friday evening. My brown cotton dress, which hung appropriately below my knees, was soaked.

"Just get in. I don't have time for *diene Kloage*—your complaints," he said, scowling.

I jumped up into the station wagon. The musty smell of the wet burlap sacks assaulted my senses.

If we were alone, I got to sit in the front seat with him and my job was to talk a lot and occasionally slap him on his legs to keep him awake. But on this evening, one of the other station workers had come into town with him, so I sat in the corner of the back of the vehicle on top of a sack of grain.

I watched the countryside roll by and daydreamed inside my own little world. I imagined that I was beautiful, with pretty new clothes and nice shoes. I imagined that I had breasts and that my bra would show through a soft white blouse, so everyone would know how grown up I was. I imagined that I had my very own room with a soft, cushy bed and deep red, velvety drapes on the windows.

I knew I wasn't supposed to be daydreaming. My mother often reprimanded me, saying that a lot of daydreaming leads to sinful behavior. I wasn't sure what she meant by this and I didn't ask. I just kept daydreaming about how beautiful my life could be.

•••

After weekends at the leprosy station, Sundays I returned to Asunción by bus. I remember a hot summer day in 1963, when I was eleven. Often, I walked the two and a half kilometers to the *Ruta*, where I would catch a bus into the city. This time my father drove me. After waiting for an hour, it was clear that we had missed the bus we were waiting for. "I'll take you to *Caacupé*," he said, which was about twenty minutes away. Sure enough, in *Caacupé*, we caught up with a city bus, ready to leave and packed solid. Sweaty bodies were crammed in on top of one another. Limbs hung out of the open windows and doors.

"*Sei gaot*—be good," he said, as he pushed me in against the bulging human mass. I caught my bag on a wooden crate carrying three chickens. A dirty, naked baby in his mother's arms tugged at my shirtsleeve. An unkempt old man rubbed himself up against my buttocks. I wanted to step out of his way, but there was nowhere to go. I wanted to tell him to stop, but I didn't know enough Spanish. Besides, I was afraid to.

As the diesel engine started up, everything jostled side to side and I fought to not lose my bearings, standing with my feet far apart for stability. I looked out through the dust-covered, large, flat rear window of the bus just in time to see Dad's brown station wagon disappearing over the hill behind us. Tears spilled out of my eyes and landed on my shirt. *I hate those chickens. I wish they would quit squawking. And how do I get my body away from the awful man behind me?* Through my tears, I kept staring at the place where Dad's car had disappeared from view. A strong magnetic thread seemed to pull my heart along behind that brown station wagon, even after it was out of sight.

My lips silently mouthed, *Please, Daddy, let me stay home.*

•••

When I was twelve, my folks moved me to the MCC Home, a hostel sort of place where Mennonites coming from the Chaco in west Paraguay to Asunción could get a bed and food. This place was the best of all, because I was completely on my own during the school week. I still went home to the leprosy station for weekends and summer vacation.

I was part of a Christian youth group, made up mostly of missionary kids living in Asunción. There were about twenty of us, all young preteenagers and teenagers teeming with excess estrogen and testosterone. We had organized a supper-basket auction for the following week to raise money for an outing to a Baptist campground east of Asunción. The plan was to meet on Saturday afternoon at a park in *Itá Enramada*, a *barrio* (neighborhood) of Asunción bordering the Paraguay River. Each girl was to bring a basket filled with a meal. At the auction, the boys would bid on the meals, and the highest bidder got to eat supper with the girl who had prepared his basket.

I longed to eat my supper with this boy who was the son of a Baptist missionary surgeon at the *Hospital Bautista* in Asunción. His name was Clyde. He had blue eyes that twinkled, and his dimpled smile could light up a whole room. The only problem was that Clyde was in love with Diana, a pretty, petite blonde who always wore perfectly matching skirts and blouses that were store bought from the States, not homemade like my clothes. I knew Clyde didn't care about me, I knew I wasn't pretty, and I didn't have any beautiful matching skirts and blouses. But I could still daydream about him, about him choosing my supper basket.

At home at the leprosy station for the weekend before the auction, I was in a quandary about what to make for my supper basket. Since I lived at the MCC Home with no access to a kitchen I could use, it was impossible for me to prepare the basket in Asunción. I would have to make something at Km. 81 a whole week before the auction.

"Mom, all the girls will have super delicious stuff in their baskets," I wailed. "What can I possibly make a whole week ahead that will be any good next Saturday?" On and on, over and over, I moaned and complained. I couldn't sleep at night. I was obsessed with that auction and with not knowing what to make.

"I just won't go to the stupid auction," I finally yelled my last day at home before returning to the city. I slammed the kitchen door and stomped to my room at the other end of the veranda.

A few minutes later, Mom opened the door to my room. "I have an idea, Marlena. We'll make fudge for your basket. Fudge should last well for a week." Her smile seemed strained.

Fudge? Just fudge? I thought to myself. But then, Mom did make the best fudge in the world. Every Easter and every Christmas, she would make big batches of fudge to distribute to all of the leprosy patients and coworkers on the station. Mom's fudge was great. Everyone knew that.

That afternoon, Mom and I made fudge, and my spirits lifted. Every time doubts about the suitability of fudge floated through my head, I told myself, "Everyone loves Mom's fudge"—over and over and over. I needed to believe it.

Mom's fudge recipe was pretty simple. We mixed together about 2/3 cup milk, 2/3 cup cocoa, 2 cups sugar, 2 tablespoons corn syrup, and ¼ teaspoon salt (Mom never measured anything out precisely). We couldn't get corn syrup in Paraguay, but we would order it every time someone visited us from the States. Mom said it kept the fudge from getting too sugary. We cooked this mixture until we got a soft ball when we dropped some of it in cold water. Mom added some vanilla and butter and we waited for the mixture to cool a bit. The real trick was to pinpoint the right moment to begin beating it. And then to know when to stop beating it, just when the brown mass began to lose its sheen. I relied on Mom to tell me when.

"OK, now!" Mom said as I pulled the pan off the stove and began beating the fudge hard with a long wooden spoon, as hard as I could. At just the right moment, we quickly spread it all out on a baking sheet, before the whole thing turned into stiffened fudge in our pot.

This would be the best fudge ever.

I had intended to pack my fudge in a beautifully adorned basket, just to up the chances that someone would want to bid on it. But all we could find at home was an old broken-down lidded wicker basket with holes in it.

"We can patch the holes with some yarn," Mom said, undeterred. She pulled a ball of blue yarn from her sewing basket.

I watched my mother expertly weave the yarn across the holes in the basket. I was grateful, but I also had serious misgivings about this plan. I wished I could talk with Mom about how uncomfortable I was around boys. How dowdy I felt in my home-sewn hand-me-down clothes. How I never knew the right things to say.

Instead, I just watched her darning needle go in and out, in and out.

Saturday of the auction was one of those bright, slightly cool, slightly breezy winter days we'd get in August. We all wore our nicest clothes for this exciting event. I had tried to pull up my hair with a ribbon, but it kept falling out, so I left it hanging loose. I noticed Diana's perfectly coiffed, short blond hair.

We had stacked all of our baskets on a wooden table underneath a tree with long gnarly roots and heavy branches that hung low, almost to the ground. The baskets weren't labeled. There was a lot of nosing around, with the boys trying to discover who had made what basket before the auction. If the bidder guessed wrong, he risked spending the evening sharing supper with a girl he didn't like, while the girl he had his eye on would spend the evening with someone else.

As I watched the boys milling around the baskets on the table, I wondered again if it had been a big mistake to come—with the fudge. Many of the baskets were brightly colored, and some of them had fancy clasps. I had caught the aroma of fried chicken, *chipa guazú* (a rich cheesy Paraguayan cornbread), *empanadas* (spicy meat-filled turnovers), and other fragrant dishes wafting up from some of the baskets. And I had caught a glimpse of a huge slice of some kind of fruity pie. I wanted to hide my basket under the table and run.

Somehow a rumor began that we girls had switched up the baskets and packed our suppers in each other's containers. So the boys who thought they had figured it out became really confused about which ones to bid for. Our group leader held up one of the baskets to begin the bidding. When the commotion didn't quiet down, he yelled loudly, "What do you bid for this basket?" He lifted the lid and looked inside, making a show of smelling the delicious food. One of the boys started the bid off at a hundred *Guaraní* (just under a dollar at that time). The leader shook his head, saying he couldn't think of letting the basket go for such a puny amount. He reminded the boys that this was a fundraiser for our yearly outing next month. The basket eventually went for six hundred *Guaraní*.

One after another the baskets on the table were auctioned off. None of them seemed to belong to the girl the bidder thought was the owner. When the leader held my basket up, he again pretended to inhale the aroma of scrumptious food.

I heard one of the boys behind me whisper, "I think that's Diana's basket."

I stopped breathing when Clyde shouted, "Two thousand *Guaraní*!"

"Sold!" the leader proclaimed, after a few moments of silence.

I felt suddenly giddy. Why had Clyde bid on my basket? Because he thought it was Diana's? Or possibly, just possibly, because he thought it was mine? But then I thought about the fried chicken, and the *chipa guazú*, and the *empanadas*, and the pies in those other baskets, and the big hunk of fudge in mine. I turned a deep crimson shade of red, standing there awkwardly under that tree.

When Clyde discovered that the basket was mine, he looked over toward Diana with a scowl, like it was her fault. Slowly, he made his way toward me, holding my tattered old basket away from him as though it held something contagious.

My heart raced. "Hi Clyde," I said too quickly, a little out of breath.

As he opened the lid, his big blue eyes widened, fixed on the single big glob of aging, slightly dried out, week-old fudge. All he said was, "You've got to be kidding."

I wanted to die.

•••

When I reached the end of grade school, my folks decided it was time for me to go to the States for high school like all of my older siblings had done. I didn't know much about how things were going for them in the US, but I did know that they were staying with Mennonite relatives in rural Kansas and that they had attended a very conservative Mennonite high school called Berean Academy.

"I don't want to go to Berean Academy in stupid tiny Elbing, Kansas," I complained. "And I refuse to live with relatives over there that I don't even know and who won't like me."

"You don't have any choice, Marlena," Dad said. "The only possibilities for high school in Paraguay are Spanish schools in Asunción. And you don't speak Spanish."

It was true. Even though I had spent fourteen years in this country, I spoke almost no Spanish. My world, both at the leprosy station and in Asunción, had been culturally isolated. I, like most of the rest of my tribe, was a German Mennonite in a Spanish land.

"I'm going to stay in Asunción and go to a Paraguayan high school," I announced one day when Dad was in town. We were sitting on a wooden bench under the bougainvillea in the MCC Home courtyard.

He glared at me. "That's not possible," he said. "You know you can't do that with your lack of the language."

"I can understand some Spanish. And it's about time I learned it," I said, at that very moment making up my mind that this was exactly what I would do.

Dad looked at me, his most willful child, and threw up his hands. "You're the one who will have to suffer through it," he said.

•••

The following week, my folks made a special trip into Asunción to go school hunting with me. There weren't many options for getting a reasonable high school education in Paraguay in those days. I had collected information on a few schools and already knew what my choice would be. But I suspected I would get a lot of resistance.

We sat around one of the green and white vinyl-covered long tables at the MCC Home where I was living. "What do you think of the *Colegio Nacional*?" Dad asked.

"I've heard that it's not a very good school academically," I said. And then I quickly added, "I was thinking about *Liceo de San Carlos*. I know someone who went there and it's supposed to be very good."

"*San Carlos*?" Dad asked, scrunching his thick eyebrows together. "Are you telling me that you want to go to a *Catholic* school?" His voice rose sharply on the word "Catholic."

"It's a good school, Dad. Why does it matter so much to you that it happens to be Catholic? Besides..." I stopped, took a deep breath and then went on, trying to soften the edge that had crept into my voice. If I upset my father, I most certainly wouldn't get what I wanted. "Besides, it's caddy-corner across the street from the *Schülerheim*, where you want me to live." The *Schülerheim* was a German Mennonite boarding house for young people from the Mennonite colonies in the Chaco who were studying in Asunción.

Nothing Bad Between Us

Dad shook his head and looked over at my mother, who hadn't said a word. "I just can't think that it would be the Lord's will that we allow our child to attend a school that's *Catholic*," she said, raising her voice on that last word just like my dad had done.

"I imagine she won't last long anyway because of the Spanish." He spoke to her as though I wasn't in the room. "Might as well let her go there."

I wanted to hug him, but I was afraid it might cause him to rethink the outlandish thing he had just allowed, so I just mumbled "thanks," picked up the sheets of paper in front of me and left to go to my room.

❢❢❢

That first year at the high school *Liceo de San Carlos*, I did very little but study. Paraguayan high schools provided no extracurricular activities like PE or music. Our classes were all about serious subjects, like Latin, history, South American literature, those sorts of things. Since I initially understood little of what I read in Spanish, I memorized entire textbooks and then regurgitated them on the exams.

One day about six months into the school year, *La Directora*, the head nun and high school principal, called me into her office. I had no idea why, but I knew it couldn't be good. We were all afraid of her. I tried to stop my hands from shaking as I rapped on the high, solid wooden double doors to her office.

"*Venga*," she called out. "Come in." The office was dimly lit. *La Directora* sat behind her heavy dark mahogany desk, erect as a board in her starched habit. Her stare felt like knife blades shooting into my chest. On one of the office's two heavily upholstered chairs beside her desk sat *Profesor Jim*énez, my history teacher. His head was bent when I entered, exposing the shiny bald spot at the top of his head. He was staring at a blue folder in his lap.

"*Profesor Jiménez* has provided solid evidence that you cheated on his exam," she pronounced slowly, emphasizing each word. "I have no choice but to expel you. I am sorry, *Señorita Es-smeet*." (Paraguayans can't pronounce a word that begins with "s" followed by a consonant without prefacing it with "es." So my last name Schmidt was pronounced *Es-smeet*.)

I swallowed hard and glanced toward my history teacher, whose head was still bent. I thought he really liked me and that he was proud of how well I had been mastering the subject.

"*Directora... Profesor Jiménez...*" I stammered, finding no words.

"You are dismissed, *señorita*," she said, turning her attention to something else on her desk.

"*Por favor*, please. I did not cheat, *Directora*." Now the words tumbled out, grammatically incorrect, but impassioned. I could not let this happen. My dad would say, "I knew this wouldn't work," and then they would send me to Elbing, Kansas.

She held up her hand to stop me. "Show her the exam booklet and the textbook," she said to my teacher, still hunched over on the chair beside her. He slowly looked up and handed me the materials.

Suddenly I knew. "*Por favor...*" I was stammering again. But I firmly closed the exam booklet, handed my professor the open textbook and began to recite sections of it from memory.

A grin slowly spread across my dear history teacher's face as I spewed out the words verbatim from the text. He seemed as relieved as I was.

After that day, whenever I passed the *Directora*, I thought I glimpsed the faintest of smiles crossing her otherwise stern face.

CHAPTER 6:
Tasting the Forbidden Fruit (1962–1968)

The Reverend Billy Graham

———

"There is a charm about the forbidden
that makes it unspeakably desirable."

—Mark Twain

———

One stormy October evening in 1962, as thunder and lightning tore across the skies over downtown Asunción, we fought our way onto one of the teeming buses on the *Avenida Mariscal López*. Our choir was headed to the *Defensores del Chaco* soccer stadium, where the Billy Graham Crusade— we called it *El Festival de Esperanza* (Festival of Hope)—was to be held that evening.

Hundreds of churches from throughout Paraguay, including my own Mennonite church, had participated in preparing for this event. For over a year, church leaders had trained thousands of "counselors" who would help people come to Jesus and had arranged a group of several hundred of us to sing in a choir for the Festival.

At eleven, I was by far the youngest member of the choir. But when I sang those exquisite hymns, I felt like an adult. Even though there was much about Mennonites that I didn't understand and didn't like, like why it was a sin to have long beautiful hair, I loved singing in the choir of the Mennonite church in Asunción. It was my favorite pastime. When I was home at the leprosy station for weekends, I made sure I got back to the city in time to sing at the service on Sunday afternoons.

As we approached the stadium, dodging deep puddles of muddy water, we felt the electricity in the air. We were aware that there had been strong opposition to the Festival in this overwhelmingly Catholic country. In fact, to our knowledge, this was the only exception Paraguayan officials had ever made to the law banning evangelistic campaigns outside the tolerated church buildings. Protesters had organized a counterdemonstration consisting of a parade of 15,000 students and a music *fiesta*. They had also loaded two planes with tiny sacks of pepper that they were going to spread over the campaign gathering to disrupt it. But it was quite obvious to our church leaders that God was all for the Billy Graham Festival and against those who opposed it. That afternoon, in a pre-Festival briefing session, the church leaders informed us that, in response to their prayers, God had ordered the violent storm that had hit the city earlier that afternoon, scattering the parade, wrecking preparations at the fiesta site, destroying both planes, and causing the death of two people involved in the opposition. But wouldn't you know it: our God-approved Festival was scheduled to begin right on time.

Crowds poured in, filling the 20,000-seat stadium, with many attendees drenched from traveling through the rainstorm. Loudspeakers blared hymns in Spanish.

We made our way high up in the bleachers to our assigned seats. I looked around me. Our combined choir took up a whole section of the bleachers. There must have been hundreds of us. The other choir members were all much older than I. They looked very serious.

We were there to help Billy Graham save sinners.

Billy Graham's voice boomed into a loudspeaker, his interpreter following along in Spanish. He spoke of heaven. Of sin. And of forgiveness.

His sermon that night was a sharp warning of judgment to come, a trumpet call to repentance. I couldn't rip my eyes away from that intense face. His eyes were mesmerizing, his deep strong voice compelling. His words unleashed within me a kaleidoscope of fear, hope, and confusion. I was there

Nothing Bad Between Us

as a church-going choir member, not as part of the crowd that needed to find Jesus Christ as their Savior. Yet I knew at that moment that he was speaking to me. My sinfulness lay like a heavy weight on my heart. I needed to finally get rid of the hurting inside.

After the sermon, our choir sang a few more hymns. I managed to mouth the words so I wouldn't stand out, but the notes stuck in my throat.

He rose again and thundered into the microphone, "By coming forward, you're saying to God, 'I'm a sinner.' " He continued, "Tonight, accept Christ in your heart and in your life."

That was the cue for our choir to repeat over and over again the altar call song:

> *Just as I am—without one plea,*
> *But that Thy blood was shed for me,*
> *And that Thou bidst me come to Thee—*
> *O Lamb of God, I come, I come.*

> *Tal como soy Señor,*
> *sin nada que entregar*
> *mas que el corazón.*
> *Me rindo todo a ti;*
> *Tómame Señor, tal como soy.*

It was an invitation to eternal life through Jesus Christ. And when he extended the invitation, they came, thousands of them, out of the bleachers and to the center of the stadium, seeking salvation and new life from the Savior of the world.

As if possessed, I felt myself rising from my seat and making my way past my choir group and down the steps. As I moved past the other choir members, I saw the look of surprise on their faces. *This is really embarrassing*, I thought. But I kept stumbling forward.

By the time I reached the center of the stadium where the counselors were stationed to speak to people one-on-one to clarify questions and pray together, my tears flowed freely.

"Forgive me, dear God. I am a sinner, and I don't want to be," I prayed.

•••

As far back as I can remember, I knew I was a sinner and I knew I needed to be saved. At the same time, I was drawn to the forbidden, like too much daydreaming about being beautiful or about kissing a boy. By the time I was twelve, I was living without adult supervision in Asunción, making sinful behavior even more appealing and easier to access.

Elena was my best friend. Her parents were also missionaries, but they lived in the city, so she got to live at home. I liked going to her house, and I often spent the night. We would lie on our backs in her bed and whisper to each other long into the night. Mostly we talked about boys.

"My mom says I'm not allowed to kiss a boy until I'm fourteen," Elena whispered.

"I can kiss a boy any time I want," I said, "but I don't think any boy wants to kiss me."

We were silent for a bit, each of us imagining our version of this important event. Our first kiss.

"It's the other part I wonder about, the stuff that happens after the kissing," I said.

Whispering even more quietly, I told Elena all about what I had learned about sexual body parts. Sometimes when I was at the leprosy station for weekends, and when I was sure no one was at home, I would crouch down in the corner where Dad often sat hunched over his shortwave radio at night, listening to the *Voice of America* broadcast from Washington DC. My interest in his office lay on the bottom bookshelf, where there sat a whole row of his fat medical books with long Latin words and graphic pictures of all things to do with human anatomy.

"So that's how I know all about penises, testicles, sperm, vulvas, menstrual blood, vaginas, all that stuff. Just ask me. I can tell you all about them. I'm just not sure how they all work together."

Elena's eyes were wide with wonder. "Did your dad ever catch you looking at pictures of penises?" she asked. "My parents would be really mad at me."

"No. I made sure he was never at home when I did that," I said, feeling good that I could contribute to our collective knowledge about boys' and girls' private body parts.

•••

Elena and I and a few other friends soon began to write our love stories down and share them amongst us. It was as though we had our own romance novel literary society. I carefully hid my box of stories under my narrow hard bed at the MCC Home.

"Listen to this," Elena said, excited about her latest chapter: *Tom and Sue were locked in an embrace under a shady tree. Sue closed her eyes and felt his lips on hers. They kissed long and hard.*

There were only so many ways we could describe long hard kisses, so the stories became fairly repetitive. But we loved each one. And those stories kept us tightly linked in our secret society.

One morning, we young authors were called to the principal's office. We were giggling when we approached her office but stopped short when we entered. The principal was sitting stiffly behind her desk. In front of her were piles and piles of our precious stories. And in straight hard chairs around her desk sat all of our parents. My mother's eyes were on the floor, as though she was the humiliated one. My father stared at me with accusing eyes.

"We've called you in here to find out about this nonsense you've been writing about," the principal said, glaring at each of us, one at a time, over her wire-rimmed reading spectacles. "Which of you is responsible for this?"

We said nothing, just stared at the piles of stories. *How did they find them? Who ratted on us? What're they going to do with our precious stories?* I wondered.

"If you don't speak up, all of you will bear the punishment," she finally said.

We said nothing.

"Alright. You will all stay after school for two hours every afternoon for the next two weeks. You will be given notebooks. During those two-hour time periods, you will write in your notebooks, *I will keep my mind free of sinful thoughts and words*. You will write this sentence over and over until your time is up. The next day you write the same sentence again, every day, until your detention period ends. Is this understood?"

She rose to dismiss us.

"I told you daydreaming leads to sin," scolded my mother as my folks pushed me along out of the office and toward their station wagon parked in front of the school.

•••

Mennonites don't dance. Or at least they didn't when I was young. Sometimes, when I would hear snatches of secular music on a radio, my body wanted to move to the rhythmic sound. But I knew that this would lead to something sinful, so I stopped. I was never really sure what sorts of sinful things would result from dancing, but I figured maybe it had to do with boys kissing girls. On the mouth.

What Mennonite youth in Asunción did, every Sunday evening following the afternoon church service, instead of dancing was something called *Bonsch*. In preparation for the *Bonsch*, we formed a large circle of folding chairs on the grounds of the MCC Home. A few people brought their instruments and played guitar and accordion. We all sat in the circle, maybe thirty to forty of us, singing *Deutsche Volkslieder* (German folk songs). One young man after another would rise and approach a young woman's chair and bow slightly. She would take his arm, and very slowly each pair would walk around in the circle, one pair following the other like a slow march, singing songs like:

> *Das Wandern ist des Müllers Lust,*
> *Das Wandern!*
> *Das muß ein schlechter Müller sein,*
> *Dem niemals fiel das Wandern ein,*
> *Das Wandern.*

Roughly translated:

> *The miller's joy is wandering,*

Is wandering!
A miller surely loses face
When staying at the same old place,
Not wandering!

Hardly romantic songs. But it all felt oh-so-romantic at the time. At the end of each song, the young man would lead his girl back to her seat and be seated himself. We would then begin singing another folk song and it would start all over again.

I was seventeen when Helmut Thiessen bowed in front of my chair at *Bonsch* one steamy, hot Sunday evening. That night I had left my wild, unruly hair loose down my back. My thin white cotton dress hung properly below my knees, but it showed just a bit more of my bare arms than was decent.

Helmut had been the first serious boyfriend of my very best girlfriend Elena for over a year. In our Mennonite circle, having a serious boyfriend was OK as long as the couple indulged in nothing more than light kissing. But Elena had left six months ago to continue her schooling in Canada and everyone assumed that their relationship had ended. I wasn't sure.

I took his arm, he pulled me close, closer than normal, and a little shiver ran down my spine. We walked in the circle and we sang. We sat down. At the next song, he bowed in front of my chair again. And then again.

Helmut was handsome in a very Germanic way. Tall and slender, with broad shoulders and wavy brown hair combed back from his prominent forehead. He was only twenty-three but he already walked with long, confident strides that reminded me of my father. By the end of *Bonsch* that evening, my knees went weak when I felt his eyes on me. I wondered if this was what it was like to be in love.

As people were leaving, Helmut roared toward me on his black BMW motorcycle and asked me to get on. I thought about Elena. I wondered what she would do if she were in my place. I didn't know what to do but decided it couldn't hurt to go for a ride with him.

Across town, he parked the motorcycle at the plaza in front of the *Catedral Basílica de la Virgen*. We walked across the plaza, my heels clattering against the cobblestones, to the low stone wall bordering the *Río*

Paraguay. A soft breeze was blowing across the river, easing the intense heat of the day.

He pulled me against his chest. I was in two-inch heels, so my head came just to the crook of his neck.

"What about Elena?" I asked in my most matter-of-fact voice that cracked despite my best efforts.

"She chose Canada over me," he said, squeezing me harder.

Then he cupped my face in his hands and kissed me. My heels lifted off the pavement, and my heart pounded against his. My first kiss was ever so much sweeter than anything I had ever imagined in my daydreams.

Within a few weeks, I became "Helmut's girl." At *Bonsch*, he bowed only in front of me and after *Bonsch* we would sit on a bench somewhere, or on a blanket on the ground, or in the back of a movie theater, and we would kiss.

I was in love. He wanted me. He cared for me.

My parents were in the US at this time, again raising money for the leprosy work, so they were largely unaware of my new boyfriend. And Elena? I had written her several times to ask her about her relationship with Helmut, but she never responded. Helmut assured me that she wasn't planning to return to Paraguay, that they were done.

One weekend, a few months into our relationship, Helmut traveled with a group of guys to east Paraguay to play soccer against the *Frieslander* team. At a volleyball game a few days after they returned, one of the guys recounted their experiences in Friesland.

"We played better than we ever have. Helmut scored the winning goal. You should have seen him," he told me.

"That's great," I said. "I haven't seen Helmut since you got back. Where is he?"

"I think he's still recovering," he said. "We went a little crazy and drank way too much. By the end of the night, we were stumbling along the road between the bar and our hotel, singing loudly. It was pretty funny, really, until Helmut and a few of the others started puking in the street."

My boyfriend? Drunk? Puking in the street?

I said nothing and left the group. I felt shaky, even a bit dizzy. I needed time to think. I had never, ever had a drink. I believed it was sinful to drink.

Nothing Bad Between Us

And my boyfriend had gotten puking drunk?

I wrote Helmut a long letter, explaining that we were through. *I can't even imagine being with someone who would do such a thing*, I wrote.

Helmut came to see me the day after receiving my letter. When he saw my red and swollen eyes, he looked contrite, but also a little confused. "Marlena, be reasonable. I just got drunk. I didn't do anything wrong."

"Just got drunk? Didn't do anything wrong?" I slammed the door in his face. I was completely unaware of the gross inconsistency in my attitudes about sin. I indulged in what I knew were sinful behaviors: daydreaming, wearing makeup, and even deep kissing a boy. But I turned into a pious Mennonite when it came to alcohol.

Helmut left, and I never backed down from my self-righteous position. Just a few months later, I heard that Elena was returning to Paraguay and that she and Helmut planned to be married.

CHAPTER 7:
Disowned (1968–1970)

My dad: What was I if he left me?

———

"And what if—what are you if the
people who are supposed to love you
can leave you like you're nothing?"

—Elizabeth Scott, *The Unwritten Rule*

———

I was seventeen, still hurting from the break-up with Helmut just months earlier, when his older brother Hans's flashy red Chevy stopped late one night in front of my *pensión*, a boarding house in Asunción where I then lived.

Earlier that day, Helmut had married my former best friend Elena. I didn't want to watch her marry my first love. But I knew I had to go. As a deeply religious ceremony, Mennonite weddings are typically performed in front of the full congregation. In our closely knit community, my absence would spark lots of gossip. I wasn't sure what Elena knew about Helmut and me. But I figured she knew something, because she had avoided me since returning from Canada.

Elena's father walked her up the aisle to the front of the sanctuary, where Helmut stood waiting for her. He was grinning. He wore a dark suit and a starched white shirt. Elena wore a plain white dress with a white covering on her head. She carried a bouquet of simple flowers. After a brief sermon, the couple exchanged written vows.

When the bride and groom shared a kiss, I stared down at my fists, tightly clenched in my lap. I heard the whoosh of Elena's dress as they passed by my pew on their way out of the church. I raised my head just as the bride and groom's family members began to walk down the aisle. Hans's eyes met mine when he passed by me. *Why is he looking at me?* I wondered.

•••

Hans rang the bell at the gate of the *pensión*. I walked out into the courtyard, wearing a long, yellow flannel nightgown with a big black shawl wrapped tightly around my shoulders.

"Marlena, *daut deit mie sao leit*—I am so sorry," he said in *Plautdietsch* through the bars of the gate.

I hardly knew this man, other than the fact that he was Helmut's brother. I knew that he was much older, maybe twenty-eight or so, and married with two kids. *What was he doing at my pensión?* "Hans, what are you doing here? How did you even know where I live?" I blurted out, confused.

"I saw how sad you were, sitting in church today. I thought you might like to go for a ride. Come."

"I'm not dressed. I can't," I said, hardly believing I heard him correctly.

"You're fine. It's OK," he said gently, reaching one hand toward me through the bars.

I stepped back. *Who was this man and why was he here? Did he really just want to comfort me?* I did long for that comfort.

I got into his car that night. He drove around the streets of Asunción. I sat stiffly in the passenger seat, pressed against the door.

"I'm really very sorry about Helmut marrying Elena. I know that you were Helmut's girl," he said, glancing at my rigid body.

Why was he saying this to me? I thought. *What would he think if he knew that I was the one who broke up our relationship? That I was the one who dumped his brother, my first boyfriend?*

Out loud I said, "*Ja*, it hurts. Thank you for caring."

I got into that flashy car many times over the course of the following months. Hans was not as handsome as his younger brother. He was shorter and stockier, with thinning hair. But I never thought about that. He was good to me. He took me for drives in the country. He took me out for ice cream. We drank *tereré* (a Paraguayan tea sipped through a metal straw from a gourd that is refilled with water and passed around from person to person) in the back room of his tire store.

•••

The front of Hans's tire store was brightly lit. Two desks sat side by side, a few cards and sheets of paper neatly stacked on the corner of one of them. Hans led me past the desks to the dark and dingy back room. The sweet, acrid smell of grease and rubber hung in the air. Piles of tires stacked all the way up to the ceiling lined the walls. In the back corner stood a small table with two chairs.

"No one will bother us here today," he said, pouring yerba tea into the gourd. "My workers have the day off. You can stay for a while, *ja*?"

"I can stay," I said, sipping on the *tereré*. I smiled at him. We had met like this for months, just to talk and drink *tereré* together. I was flattered that someone so old and sophisticated would think of me as such a good friend.

He reached across the table to touch my hand. It felt like my stomach did a somersault and the room began to spin. I pinched my eyes shut tight, trying to steady myself. And then I felt his breath on my face and his lips brushing lightly against mine.

"Hans, what are you doing?" I gasped.

He was pulling me to my feet. "I've wanted to do this for so long, Marlena. I love you."

I wanted to respond to his love, but his tongue in my mouth felt like a massive foreign object. I pushed him away.

"I'm sorry," Hans said, taking both of my hands in his. "I didn't mean to take this too fast."

"I'm sorry, too," I said, not knowing what else to say.

For the next few weeks, Hans dropped light kisses on my lips every time we met. He held me in his arms. I grew more comfortable within the safe circle of his love for me.

"Come," he said hoarsely one day after we had been cuddling in the back of his store. He pulled me along behind him toward his car.

We drove to the outskirts of Asunción. He seemed so certain about where he was going. I sat next to him, flushed, slightly dizzy, looking out the side window and seeing nothing.

He pulled in next to a house that looked abandoned. The windows were boarded up, and the brick walkway up to the front door was broken down. Hans unlocked the door and led me inside, locking the door carefully behind him. The house contained just two adjoining rooms and an outhouse. The only furniture was a bed in the middle of one of the rooms, covered with a grimy-looking bedspread. The air smelled sour and stale.

Hans pulled me onto the bed, held my face in his hands and kissed me gently. "I want to love you like you've never been loved before," he whispered in my ear.

He undressed me and then stood back to admire what he saw. "*Du best soo aus eene Popp*—you're just like a doll," he said.

I sucked in my breath when he pulled down his pants. Dad's medical books didn't have any pictures of penises like this. It was monstrously huge, and instead of hanging between Hans's legs, where I thought penises were supposed to be, it poked straight out from his body. I shrank away from him.

Sensing my fear, he said ever so gently, "It's OK, Marlena. We'll take it slowly."

"Wait, wait," I cried. "I don't want to get pregnant. We can't do this."

"Trust me," he said, cradling me in his arms. "I will pull out of you and do it in a way that makes sure you will not get pregnant."

•••

In November of that year, I graduated from my high school, *Liceo de San Carlos*. I was home at the leprosy station for summer vacation. It had been about eleven months since Hans first showed up at my *pensión*.

In the weeks following my high school graduation, I became so sick I could no longer keep food down and pain ripped through my vagina every time I peed. In order to keep this mysterious condition from my parents, I ran outside after almost every meal and vomited behind the hedge near the veranda of our house. My body seemed to be falling apart in other ways as well. I had lost a lot of weight in the past two months and I was bleeding vaginally.

Terrified that I was dying, I took a bus into Asunción and checked myself into the *Hospital Bautista*. An overweight woman in a starched white uniform and a stiff nursing cap ushered me into an examination room. The strong smell of chemical disinfectants assaulted my senses. The nurse asked me to undress and pointed to the examining table.

"Please lie here and put your feet up in these stirrups," she said.

I turned toward the wall and shut my eyes tight when the doctor entered the room. "Let's take a look," he said, pulling up a stool and seating himself between my spread legs. He pushed my knees farther apart. My body began to shake, and I let out a thin wail when his ice-cold instrument penetrated my burning vagina.

As abruptly as he had entered, the doctor left the room without a word. The overweight nurse asked me to get dressed. I sat in a chair, hunched over my aching body, and waited.

After what seemed like hours, the doctor called me into his little office cubicle. He settled into his chair across the desk from me, in his starched white coat and wire-rimmed spectacles. "Marlena, you are pregnant, and I believe you have an advanced case of gonorrhea, although I am sending a specimen to the lab to confirm this. I am hospitalizing you until you are stable. You're barely eighteen. I have to let your parents know. Please tell me who the father of this baby is and how this happened."

I stared at his wire-rimmed spectacles. *Gonorrhea? What was that? Pregnant? How could I be pregnant?* Hans had promised me that we would never risk pregnancy.

●●●

I was lying in the hospital bed, an IV stuck in my arm, when Mom and Dad walked through the door. After a first glance, I turned my head away from them. I couldn't look them in the eyes. Mom's face was puffy and red from crying, and Dad's eyes were clouded with fury.

"I...I'm..." My voice cracked.

"We've spoken with the doctor. Get some sleep. We'll be back tomorrow," Dad said. They turned and walked out.

After my parents left, late in the evening when few people were around, Hans appeared in my semi-dark hospital room. His face was set in a severe grimace and his voice was flat and business-like. He stood beside my bed, but he didn't look me in the eyes.

"I'll pay for an abortion. I know someone who can take care of this."

I heard a voice that sounded like a stranger's from deep inside of me scream, "Get out of this room. Get away from me!"

As Hans strode out of the room, his words echoed in my head and I shuddered. *An abortion? Only sinful women of the world do stuff like that,* I thought. A broken sob caught in my throat when the realization hit me that night, lying alone in my hospital bed: *I am one of those women.*

●●●

After a few more tests that confirmed the gonorrhea, it turned out that I might also have a large tumor in my abdomen, requiring exploratory surgery after I regained sufficient strength. The doctor sent me home on antibiotics for a few weeks.

A strained and tense silence pervaded those two weeks at home at the leprosy station before the surgery. I wanted to ask Dad about the gonorrhea, but I didn't dare. *What was it? How did I get it? Why did I get it?* I knew it had something to do with my affair, with the sex, but the doctor in Asunción had been vague about it. Finally, one afternoon when I was alone at home, I flipped through my father's medical tomes on the bottom shelf of his office. There it was. *Gonorrhea: An infection caused by a kind of bacteria that is passed during sexual contact. The infection is easily spread and occurs most often in people who have many sex partners.*

Many sex partners? Many sex partners? I swallowed hard, closed the book, and sat back on my heels. *Was it possible that I was only one of many?* My stomach began to convulse, and I ran outside to vomit.

• • •

One morning a few days later I overheard Dad's long prayers, as he and Mom and my younger siblings sat around the breakfast table. I refused to sit at the table with them and was squatting on the lowest step of the concrete stairs leading down from our veranda. It was still early morning, but the cicadas were chirring, and the heat was already suffocating.

I heard him solemnly name the members of our family, beseeching the Lord to bestow health and blessings on each one. "Lord, we ask that Thou mightest richly bless John Russell, Elisabeth, Wesley and David in Kansas, and also…" He went from oldest to youngest, as was his custom. But he didn't name me.

I huddled lower on the step, clasping both arms around my knees. When his prayer ended and they rose from the table, I ran to my room.

I lay on my bed with my hands on my belly. *Certainly, I wasn't someone who deserved the Lord's blessing. But was I doubly cursed? Was there a married man's baby in there as well as a cancerous growth? What would I do with this baby? What would I do if I had cancer?* The questions were so overwhelming that I couldn't focus my mind. For the first time I could remember, I had no plan to get out of the mess I had created. I turned over on the bed and pushed my face into the hard pillow.

Mom rapped on the door. When I said nothing and didn't move, she came in. "Marlena, you need to eat something," she said softly. "You need to build up your strength for the surgery."

"I'm not hungry," I mumbled into my pillow.

"Please, honey…" She began to cry and left the room.

I just kept pushing my head against the hard pillow, my eyes pinched shut against the world. I hated that Mom was acting like nothing had happened. Like I should just sit down at the table with them and eat. Like this was a day like any other.

A week passed. I ate almost nothing, said almost nothing, and spent almost all of my time in my bedroom, trying to figure out what I could possibly do with my life. One afternoon, there was a loud banging on my door. Dad walked briskly into the room.

"Get yourself out of that bed right now, Marlena. If you don't want to eat, that's fine, but you're going to make yourself useful. Get out of here and start helping with the chores. Now." His voice held a bitter edge.

"I'm not getting up," I said, wishing even as I said it that I had said something else, anything else.

He grabbed my arm and pulled me off the bed, dragging me behind him, out onto the veranda.

"Let go of me," I screamed.

My mother came out of the kitchen, her face drawn with concern.

"John..." her voice faded.

Still gripping my arm, Dad's voice exploded in a sharp staccato. "*There. Are. Plenty. Of. Other. Children. To. Love. I. Don't. Need. You. I. Want. You. Out. Of. My. Life.*" His nostrils spread wide and taut.

The weight of Paraguay's humid, stifling, late afternoon November heat fell heavily on the three of us standing in an awkward semicircle on the open veranda of our house. My light cotton shift dress stuck to my sticky, sweaty skin. I glanced up from the floor and saw my mother's stooped figure, her eyes turned down, her neck muscles pulsing. I looked back down and saw her toes, with those dirty, unkempt toenails, moving in a nervous rhythm up and down in her flip-flops. Up and down. Up and down. No one said another word.

I started back toward the girls' bedroom, ten or so meters toward the far end of the veranda. Halfway there, I felt the by-now familiar heaving of my stomach and leaned over the banister to throw up. My entire body began to shake. Acid still stinging in my throat, I stumbled the rest of the way to the girls' room.

I heard the kitchen door close. Was I supposed to pack a suitcase? But I had nowhere to go and no money to get me there and a baby and some sort of weird tumor in my belly. So I sat on the hard bed in my room and stared out the window until the final rays of sun vanished and the welcome darkness

Nothing Bad Between Us

enveloped me. The cicadas' songs outside my window were beginning to fade. I heard the clattering of dishes in the kitchen at the other end of the veranda, I smelled the familiar pungent smell of the kerosene lamps being lit, and I strained to hear the murmur of my parents' voices. But they didn't come for me and I didn't leave my room.

I did not move out, just made myself as invisible as I could, avoiding contact as much as possible with my parents and younger siblings. The surgery date was still a week away. I hid out in my bedroom during most of that week, haunted by that familiar feeling that I was once again an extra, unwanted person, this time in my own home. Since my body could hardly keep down any food, I refused to come to the table at mealtimes. For hours each day, I sat at the edge of my bed, my arms wrapped around my body, rocking back and forth, thinking about the mess I had made of things and wondering what was to become of my life.

•••

The day of my surgery, Dad drove me to the hospital. His jaw was set. He said nothing.

"Dad, I'm scared," I said, trying not to sound too desperate. "Someone is about to cut me open and that really scares me. Can you please come with me into that operating room when he cuts me open?" Despite everything, my father was still a heroic doctor in my mind.

I saw him stiffen in the seat beside me. I waited, hardly breathing. Finally, he barely nodded.

•••

My mother was sitting beside my hospital bed when I awoke from the anesthesia.

"Am I... Was I..." I groaned. Pain washed over me and dragged me back deep into a blessed dark, empty place.

When I awoke the second time, the single burning question in my mind came together more clearly.

"No. You are not pregnant, Marlena," Mom said, tears welling up in her eyes.

I touched my bandaged belly gingerly, carefully. *There was no baby in there. I wasn't pregnant.* The thought that I might have had a cancerous tumor never occurred to me. All I could think about was that I wasn't pregnant.

I drifted back to sleep.

"Marlena, the doctor wants to talk to you about the tumor." Mom was gently tapping me on the shoulder to awaken me. "He's here now."

The surgeon pulled up a chair next to my bed.

"Marlena, here's a photo of the mass we removed from your body." He handed me three little black and white Polaroid photographs.

"It just looks like a big blob," I said.

"Well, it's more than just a blob. Look here. You can see a deformed head, bones, teeth, hair, and fragments of a spine."

My mouth fell open and I stared at my mother. "I thought you told me I wasn't pregnant?" I cried out.

"Marlena, listen to me. You weren't...you aren't pregnant. This is not your baby. This is your twin." I tried to interrupt him, but the doctor continued. "As far as we can tell, back when you and your twin were conceived, both of the fetuses shared the same placenta, but apparently you wrapped yourself around it and enveloped it. In response, it became a parasite by drawing on your blood supply. Its survival depended on your survival. It had no brain and lacked internal organs, so it was unable to survive on its own."

"What are you talking about?" I didn't understand.

"You carried your twin around in your abdomen and until you reached puberty, it probably remained very small. With you now at age eighteen, it had grown, and it squashed your stomach and intestines to where they could no longer hold your food," he said patiently.

I turned toward the wall. *This can't be happening to me,* I thought. *I'm not only a sinner. I'm a freak.*

The surgeon cleared his throat. "I have something else I need to tell you—" he began.

"I have cancer," I interrupted, almost matter-of-factly.

My mother rushed over to my side. "No, you don't, honey. No pregnancy. No cancer." She took my hand in both of hers.

Nothing Bad Between Us

"The mass had wrapped itself around both of your ovaries, clinging to them for its survival. I had to remove your entire right ovary."

I stared at him, not knowing what I was supposed to say about that.

He continued. "When I moved to the other side to cut out your left ovary, your father asked me to carve around it, removing what I had to, but leaving a tiny remaining portion of your left ovary intact."

"So, what are you saying?" This all seemed so strange. And besides, what I really wanted to concentrate on was that I wasn't pregnant.

"I'm saying there's probably not enough ovary there for you to ever get pregnant, but your father thought it might give you at least a chance."

"Where's Dad?" I asked, noticing for the first time that he wasn't in the room.

"He had to return to the leprosy station to take care of a medical emergency, but he stayed with you all through the surgery," Mom said.

I looked over at my mother, hunched beside my bed, still holding onto my hand, and then at the surgeon, wondering how I was supposed to react to the news about this twin and the whole ovary situation. I really didn't want to think about any of it.

"I need to sleep now," I said.

•••

A few weeks later, I was convalescing back at the leprosy station. Christmas was just around the corner. I wanted to be excited about my favorite holiday, but even putting the Christmas tree together brought little joy.

"Marlena, the Mennonite minister from the Asunción church has come out to see you," my mother said one morning, as I sat on our red vinyl sofa, listlessly staring at the Christmas tree.

Pastor Arnold Entz stood in the doorway. "*Goondach*—Good day," he said, coming into the room.

" '*N'dach*," I said, staring at his face and then my mother's, wondering what was going on.

My mother left and Pastor Entz sat down beside me.

"How is the healing coming along?" he asked awkwardly.

"Fine."

"Marlena." He paused and took a deep breath. "There will be a special meeting of the congregation to discuss your transgressions with Hans Thiessen and to determine the consequences. You will be asked to confess your sins. The meeting is taking place the first Sunday of the new year, January 4th, right after our regular church service."

"What...how...I mean...who knows about this? And who told you?" My face felt like it was burning, and my scar pulsed with pain.

"Annaliese, one of the nurses at the *Hospital Bautista*, has brought all of it to our attention. And we now need to address the matter in our congregation."

I stared at him, not knowing what to say.

"*Daut deit mie leit*—I am sorry, Marlena." He rose and left the room.

•••

I had wanted to put the whole experience behind me, the twin, the presumed pregnancy, my dad disowning me, Hans, everything. But on that blisteringly hot day of January 4, 1970, I was forced to revisit all of it when I was called to repent publicly in front of the congregation of my church in Asunción. My pious accusers still thought I was pregnant, because that's what Annaliese, the Mennonite nurse, had told Pastor Entz.

As I stumbled out of the side door of the church into the stifling afternoon heat, branded unclean, I wondered how I would ever again face those people.

CHAPTER 8:
My Escape (1970)

Desperate to escape at nineteen

_____

"Desperation is the raw material of drastic change. Only those who can leave behind everything they have ever believed in can hope to escape."

—William S. Burroughs

_____

I lost all interest in socializing during the months following the church sanction. I rarely went to church and, when I did, I would sit near the back of the sanctuary, fleeing right after the service. The *Bonsch* gatherings of the Mennonite young people no longer held any appeal.

But I refused to give up on my lifelong dream of becoming a medical doctor like my father. Before graduating from high school, I had made arrangements to study with a tutor, whom everyone in the Paraguayan medical community called *La Doctora*, in preparation for the medical school entrance exams. I was going to study medicine at the *Facultad de Medicina* in Asunción.

Every morning, I boarded one of the *micros*, VW vans that served as minibuses throughout Asunción. I walked the five blocks from the *micro* stop to the home of *La Doctora*. Everything in her house was overstuffed: the drapes, the cushions, the couches. *La Doctora* harmonized well with her overstuffed home surroundings, her obese body draped in long flowing gowns.

I walked through her congested house, out to the back patio, and up a narrow flight of concrete steps to a dark little room with a row of hard wooden chairs. There I sat all day, along with a few other students, in front of the chalkboard. *La Doctora*, her hands white with chalk dust, drew endless chains of molecules and polymers and sketched monomers within copolymers. I was like a sponge, taking in every detail and absorbing the arcane languages of biology, chemistry, and anatomy.

And I continued to yearn for what I had lost. When I wasn't memorizing formulas, I thought about Hans, wondering what he was doing, wondering why he had betrayed me.

One cold and drizzly July afternoon, I ran through the rain to catch a *micro* to go home. I had spent six hours with *La Doctora*, memorizing the periodic table of elements and learning which elements have identical valance electron configurations.

My head hurt. The rain had begun to come down harder and had soaked through my light rain jacket and blouse. No *micro* was anywhere in sight.

I stopped at the corner of the cobblestone street, muddy water pooling at my feet and seeping into my shoes. *What am I doing?* I said aloud to no one. *Whose dream was it that I become a medical doctor? Dad's or mine?* With more determination than I had mustered since my world began to crumble about a year ago, I walked the twenty or so blocks back to my *pensión*, holding my head high in the pouring rain.

The hardest part was telling Dad. I kept thinking about what he had said when I told him I wanted to study medicine. "You'll make a fine doctor, Marlena." His eyes had been filled with pride.

One early evening when my father stopped to see me at the end of one of his Asunción shopping trips for the leprosy station, I blurted it out. "Dad, I can't live in Asunción any more. I'm done with *La Doctora*. I don't even think I want to be a doctor. I don't know what I want. I just want out."

"What do you mean, 'you want out'?" he asked, his brow furrowing.

Nothing Bad Between Us

"I don't know, Dad. I just know that I can't go on like this anymore. Maybe I should try to go to school somewhere else. Maybe in the States." The idea hadn't occurred to me until that moment. I had no money. How would that even be possible? Where would I go? Would my folks pay for me to go?

"I can't believe you want to just quit, throw away all of the hard work, walk away from it," he said. His voice, at that moment laced with disappointment, stung worse than any physical lashing of his ever had.

My folks determined that I was too emotionally unstable to go to the States alone, unless I went to a small Mennonite college in Newton, Kansas. If I went to Bethel College, they figured, my Mennonite relatives would surround me. They might save me from myself.

"I refuse to go to Bethel," I protested. "I wouldn't fit in at all." Going to a small conservative Mennonite school felt like walking back into a trap.

"If we pay for you to go to the States, you'll go to Bethel," my dad said brusquely.

I had no choice. It was my ticket out. Maybe it would end up being a ticket right back into what would be another hellhole for me, but I had to take that chance. I agreed to go to Bethel College. My folks contacted Uncle Herb, my dad's oldest brother, who lived in Newton. They explained the circumstances and asked him to keep an eye on me.

•••

In August of 1970, at nineteen, I packed my few belongings into a large duffel bag. Most of the bag I filled with *yerba mate*, the Paraguayan tea I thought I couldn't live without.

I watched the familiar neighborhoods whizz by as we made our way to the *Puerto Presidente Stroessner* airport. Dad drove. My mother sat quietly beside him. I was in the back seat, my duffel bag by my side. Occasionally I saw Dad's mouth in the rearview mirror, pressed into a thin tight line.

I closed my eyes, hardly believing I was really leaving home. I wished I knew what Mom and Dad were thinking. I wanted them to talk to me. I wanted them to tell me that they would miss me. But they remained silent.

Dad parked the car, and the three of us walked into the terminal together.

I dragged my green duffel bag along on the ground behind me.

"Here's your ticket," Dad said. "And here's Uncle Herb's phone number in case you need to call him. He said you can call him collect."

I looked at him, confused.

"Calling collect means that you call an operator, who will call Uncle Herb's number. And he'll pay for it."

He gave me a quick hug and stepped aside. I turned toward Mom, my eyes filling with tears.

"You are a sick child. I pray that you will find your way," she said, embracing me.

•••

As the Braniff International Airways flight banked over the red tile roofs of Asunción and headed north, I dropped my head into both hands and sobbed. The same paradoxical push-pull that had characterized my whole life sliced through me: I wanted to escape, and at the same time I wanted desperately to stay.

The captain's announcements crackled through the cabin and I raised my head. The stewardess came by to ask if she could help. A hot pink and purple mini dress barely concealed her model-like body, and her shiny black hair was coiffed into a flawless bob with perfect bangs. I felt like pulling on them to see if it was a wig. I looked down at my homemade blue bell-bottom pants and the blue and white checkered shirt that didn't quite match, both of which my mother had sewn for this journey to the United States. I had seen wide-legged pants like these in an American magazine and thought for sure they would make me fit in. Now I was no longer so sure.

"I'm fine," I answered, turning toward the window and through my tears smiling my most grown-up, confident smile.

At the Miami airport, large men in khaki pants and brown shirts covered with badges checked everyone's documents and rummaged through some people's luggage. When they got to my tattered canvas bag, four of them huddled together saying stuff I couldn't quite hear, occasionally nodding or shaking their heads.

"You'll need to step over here and wait," one of them said. I stared at him blankly. I understood English, but he must not have been sure. He repeated in Spanish, "*Espera aquí. ¿Tiene su pasaporte?*" He took my passport and left.

I ran after them. "Wait. Where are you taking my bag and my passport?" I called out.

A large woman stepped out from behind a counter that had a big sign over the top that said "Passport Control" in large capital letters. Her orange hair was piled high on her head like a shiny haystack.

"They need to analyze the contents of your bag, miss," she said as she approached me. "You need to wait here. This is where they'll be bringing it back to you." Her eyes seemed kind.

"OK. Thank you," I mumbled, wondering why they had chosen my bag to "analyze."

After about an hour, I walked up to the "Passport Control" lady with the orange haystack hair. "I need to get on a plane to fly to a city called Houston. And then I need to get on another plane to go to someplace called Wichita." She raised her eyebrows questioningly. "The problem is, the plane to Houston is leaving in half an hour. I don't know what to do."

"You will miss that flight to Houston," she said. "Do you have someone you can call?"

I fished the piece of paper with Uncle Herb's number out of my pocket and handed it to her. "I need to call him collect. Can you help me?"

She pointed to a red booth across the room. "There's a pay phone. You just dial "O" to get the operator."

I heard a ringing sound after the operator dialed Uncle Herb's number. Once. Twice.

"*Ja*, hello?" It sounded so much like Dad's voice I wanted to cry.

"Will you accept a collect call from someone named Marlena Schmidt?" the operator asked.

"Well yes, I suppose so," the clipped dad-voice said.

"Hello, Uncle Herb. This is Marlena," I said, my voice quivering slightly.

"Yes, I know that," he said. "What's going on?"

I tried to explain the situation.

"Make sure you get someone to help you book a new set of flights," he said. "And call me back when you know what flights you'll be on. Susan will be picking you up in Wichita."

"Susan...?" I asked.

"Your cousin. Susan's my daughter, remember?"

I didn't. I knew I had lots of cousins in the US, but I didn't remember their names.

•••

I sat on the floor, my back against the wall. I watched people coming and going. Everyone seemed to be in a hurry. I fought back tears. I had been excited about seeing Uncle Herb. I remembered him from his visits to Paraguay. But he sounded cold, uninterested over the phone. Was I marked as a no-good sinner even here in the US?

One of the officers who had taken my bag came back to chat with the "Passport Control" lady and said in a voice loud enough for me to hear. "People like that shouldn't be allowed to enter our country. Did she think she could get away with this?"

I stared at them both, not registering what he had just said. Suddenly I panicked. Did they think I was a bandit of some kind? This was all a big mistake. I stumbled to my feet and ran toward them.

"I'm not a bandit. I have parents in Paraguay who do important work for the Lord. They've sent me to go to school..." I felt no qualms about pulling out the God card if it would help me get out of this mess.

The orange haystack lady held up both hands. "Please, miss. You'll get your bags soon. Please don't make a big commotion, or you'll get yourself arrested."

"Arrested?" My eyes grew large and I slumped silently back onto the floor.

I closed my eyes and took a deep breath. *When would Mom and Dad find out if I was suddenly surrounded by those gunmen and taken away? What if they decided to shoot me? What if I died here?*

I stared in dismay at the hamburgers, chips, sodas, and cookies people were consuming as they walked past me. My stomach rumbled. Even though I was free to walk around to find food, I had no American money. Eventually,

I fell into an intense fog, barely registering what was happening around me.

A rough tap on my shoulder shook me out of my befuddled state. "You can go now," said the officer who didn't want me in the US. He handed me my scruffy bag and my documents. "We have determined that the leaves in your bag are not a drug after all."

"*Drug?*" I mumbled. "What do you mean?"

"Go on. Get your flights straightened out at that counter over there." He pointed to the far end of the concourse.

Go on, get your flights? That was it, after spending six hours waiting for my bag? I wanted to ask them why they had done this to me, but they had already turned to leave. So, new tickets in hand, I again called Uncle Herb collect and prepared to continue my journey.

•••

As I deplaned in Wichita, I wondered how Uncle Herb's daughter would know who I was. But for some reason, she seemed certain I was the one she was waiting for from the moment I walked into the terminal building. She waved at me.

Susan wore a pair of pure white shorts and a neatly pressed blouse. I looked down at my stained and crumpled blue pants and mismatched shirt and felt suddenly like the poor cousin from a third-world country that I was. My eyes scanned her perfectly manicured feet in dainty white sandals. I wondered if she even knew that there was such a thing as hookworms. Or itchy worms that sometimes lodged themselves in your butt.

"Hi, Marlena. Welcome to the States," Susan said, smiling and holding out her hand to me, her poor cousin.

"Hi. Thanks for getting me," I muttered, still eyeing her perfect feet. "Where am I going?"

"I'm supposed to take you to Uncle Art and Aunt Frieda's," she said.

I wanted to ask her why I wasn't staying with Uncle Herb. But instead I just stared at the floor in my clumsy discomfort.

Susan led the way to her car, a shiny new Chevrolet. I scanned the parking lot. Did everyone in the States drive brand-new cars?

I dropped into the passenger seat, exhausted and disoriented. And suddenly very sad. I missed the cacophony of noisy blaring horns and barking dogs, the sweet, heavy, pungent odor of tropical flora, mixed with diesel fumes and smoke and the pulsating vibrancy of the people in Asunción. The streets here were so clean. The air smelled like nothing. And no one honked.

•••

I stayed with Aunt Frieda and Uncle Art (my father's sister and her husband) for a few weeks until I was able to move into my dorm room at Bethel. For me, it was just the latest installment of "God will Provide." Even though they treated me kindly, the two weeks with them took me painfully back to those early years in Asunción, when I had been an unwanted extra person in people's homes. I vowed to do whatever it took to create my own home as soon as possible and to never again rely on strangers for a place to live.

It was a small, ranch-style home in North Newton, just a few blocks from the Bethel College campus. My Aunt Frieda, a petite white-haired lady, showed me to my borrowed room in their basement. Wide-eyed, I scanned the sparkling, sterile bathroom next to it. A pure white shag carpet lay like a sculpted necklace around the base of the toilet. Instead of the typical smell of excrement, this toilet room smelled faintly sweet, like flowers.

"Where's the bucket for the toilet paper?" I asked.

Even though we had an outdoor toilet at home on the leprosy station, I had used flush toilets in Asunción. But we never threw toilet paper into the bowl. The plumbing couldn't handle it. There was always a bucket next to the toilet for the soiled paper.

"What do you mean?" Aunt Frieda asked, eyeing me with raised eyebrows as though I were an alien from another planet.

She patiently explained to me that in the US it was OK to throw the soiled paper directly into the toilet bowl. Amazing, I thought. So that morning I happily tossed a bloody tampon into the bowl and flushed the toilet.

Glug, glug, glug.

Horrified, I watched the murky red water slowly rise, rise, rise up toward the rim of the toilet. I frantically slammed down on the flush handle, trying to stop the rising tide. The handle dangled lifelessly. The water began to spill over the side of the toilet and onto the white rug.

I ran up the stairs. "Aunt Frieda, Uncle Art, please come down. Something's wrong with the toilet," I hollered.

By the time they arrived, the dark red flood was spreading beyond the white rug and onto the shiny white tile. My uncle grabbed a short broomstick-looking thing with an inverted rubber bowl on the end and kept pushing it up and down in the bowl, causing more of the bloody mess to splash across the bathroom.

"Call a plumber," he said to my Aunt Frieda, frowning and shaking his head. "I can't believe..." He ate the rest of his words, but I had heard enough. I wanted to hide under my bed until I could escape and be alone in my dorm room.

The plumbers spent the rest of the day extricating the tampon from my relatives' pipes.

•••

Bethel College was just as bad as I had thought it would be. The students were mostly from neighboring Mennonite farm communities. I didn't try to get to know them. They all seemed to know each other. They all had lots of nice store-bought clothes. They all had parents who helped them move in and who brought them home-cooked food. I defiantly skipped most of my classes and flunked my way through the first and only semester I was there, without a thought about what I might do next.

But I loved singing in the Bethel College choir.

As the college choir's baritone soloist, Steve Fiol stood directly in front of my alto row that fall. Curly black hair fell to his shoulders. I stood close enough behind him to smell his aftershave, Old Spice I think, mingled with the faint sweet smell of tobacco.

We were practicing a jazzy cantata Dave Brubeck had composed the prior year. During a time of national polarization over the Vietnam War and the fight for equal rights, Brubeck's "Gates of Justice" was a gutsy and complex attempt to forge a common bond between the American Jewish and Black communities, both uprooted from their homelands. To illustrate the connections between the Black and Jewish groups in the civil rights movement, our choir director intentionally juxtaposed Steve's deep baritone voice to sing the most famous section of King's "I Have a Dream" speech, *Free at last! I'm free at last! Thank God Almighty, we're free at last!* and a tenor cantor to sing Hillel's Jewish proverb, *If the time for action is not now, when is it?*

I knew nothing of these social struggles in America, having just arrived. But the brilliant choral writing fired shivers up and down my spine, especially when we all sang in unison *Lord, Lord, what will tomorrow bring?*

A few weeks into the semester, Dr. Jost, the director, invited the choir members to his house for a BBQ. I was walking back to my dorm room after the event when Steve caught up with me.

"Where are you from?" he asked. I wondered why everyone always knew that I was from somewhere else.

"Paraguay," I answered, embarrassed, as I so often was about being a poor missionary kid from an unknown land.

"Really?" Steve turned toward me. For the first time I noticed the warmth of his brown eyes and the way his wavy dark hair framed his face and fell to his shoulders. "My parents are missionaries in India," he said. "That's where I grew up."

"Really? I mean..." I felt so foolish about having mimicked him. "I mean, when did you come to the States?"

"Six years ago. I was almost through college when I got drafted two years ago. Now I'm back to finish up."

"You were in Vietnam?"

"No. I lucked out. I was stationed in New York City."

We walked for a while in silence. I marveled at the neatly squared off weed-less garbage-less areas of grass in front of each house we passed.

"Do you sometimes wonder why there's no garbage in this country?" I asked, surprised that it felt OK to ask this guy a question I was sure others here would think was stupid.

He grinned at me. "Oh, there's garbage all right. People here are just really good at hiding it."

It was like coming home.

•••

Several weeks later, Steve and I were walking through the woods near the Bethel College campus, mostly quiet, holding hands. He wore his ubiquitous slim black jeans and white shirt, a green army jacket slung over his shoulder. I didn't have the money I needed to go to the secondhand store to buy myself a coat, so I shivered as the autumn breeze blew through my tattered black sweatshirt. A soggy layer of yellow maple leaves carpeted the ground. The rich scent of damp soil hung in the air. I felt his musky presence and evoked in my breath.

I stopped, looked at Steve, opened my mouth to say something, and then turned and started to walk again.

"What is it?" he asked, gently pressing my hand in his.

How can I tell him? I was beginning to love this gentle, kind man, son of missionaries in India. I had to tell him. But when he learned that I was a marked and soiled woman, would he run?

I could hear my heartbeat. "Steve, I have something I have to tell you."

He stopped and looked into my eyes, waiting.

"I had an affair with a married man in Paraguay. I was banned from singing and playing the organ in my church. I got a disease called gonorrhea..." The words fell out of my mouth like vomit.

"Wait. Stop. Slow down. Please start from the beginning. Tell me what happened," he said, a worried look, like a dark shadow, crossing his face.

I told him everything. Steve listened, occasionally asking a question. He never let go of my hand.

When I finished, he pulled me into his arms and held me there against his chest. "I'm so sorry about what you've been through, Marlena," he whispered into my ear. "I'll always be there for you." He paused and then pushed me away gently so he could look me in the eyes. "And I will always love you in the morning."

"I've never ever felt like someone would be there for me for the rest of my life," I said, tears spilling from my eyes. "I always thought I would have just me to depend on."

A few days later we lay together for the first time in his two-room pad on the outskirts of the Bethel campus. Steve had taken off his clothes and was lying on his back on the mattress in the middle of the floor. The walls were covered with Indian batiks, tacked up with thumbtacks. A candle burned in one corner of the room. He watched me as I fiddled with my clothing.

"What's wrong? Are you nervous? D'you not want to spend the night here?" he asked, pulling himself up and leaning on one elbow.

"I do want to spend the night with you, Steve. But I want you to know that I put on this panty girdle today." I pulled down my long pants and revealed the tight, binding, elastic groin guard. "And I'm going to keep it on all night. I just don't know for sure whether I'm still unclean. This isn't coming off until I know."

Steve grinned and pulled my girdle-clad body down next to him. "I'll still love you in the morning," he said.

•••

The following week, I called Uncle Herb.

"*Ja*, hello." That voice always made me flinch.

"Uncle Herb. It's Marlena." Before he had a chance to say anything, I rushed on. "I need to see you. I mean...I need to see you at your clinic. I mean...I don't know if I still have... Did my dad tell you that I had gon...?"

His gruff voice interrupted my stumbling outburst.

"Yes. I know all about your gonorrhea. And yes, we can get you checked. Come to my clinic on Monday morning. Can you be there by eight o'clock?"

"I'll be there. Thank you, Uncle Herb."

I heard the click of his phone.

•••

My shoulders hunched down and I shrank as low into my chair in the clinic waiting room as I could, hoping no one would walk in who would recognize me as John Schmidt's daughter or Herb Schmidt's niece. But it must have been before clinic hours, because I was the only one in the waiting room. A door opened and I looked up, expecting a nurse to usher me into Dr. Herb's office, like nurses always do. Instead it was Uncle Herb himself who led me into his examining room.

"OK, Marlena, get up on that examining table, and let's take a look," he said in that staccato dad-voice. His squared-off jaw was set in a face that was all about serious business.

I got up onto the examining table and squeezed my eyes shut tight as a flood of memories raced through me. I braced myself for the cold intrusion of the metal into my vagina. Less than one year ago, I had placed my feet into the same kind of stirrups. I had endured the invasion of the cold metal into my searing cervix. And the verdict had been: *Unclean*.

I pulled my breath in sharply and held it, my legs spread wide and my feet high in their stirrups. It was no longer just about me. I needed the results to free me to be in a healthy relationship with a man who loved me. For the first time, I felt the full significance of that verdict a year ago.

"Call me in a week," Uncle Herb said, pulling off his rubber gloves.

•••

"Hello?"

"Uncle Herb. It's me, Marlena."

"*Ja?*" There was a pause. "Ah, *ja*, the results." I heard him shuffle some papers on his desk. "You are clean. Your body no longer carries any traces of gonorrhea."

I began to shake.

"Marlena, did you hear me?" he asked.

"Yes, thank you," I whispered and sank into the nearest chair.

I had just been given a second chance at life.

CHAPTER 9:
The Return (1971–1972)

Bringing Steve home

———

"And bring the fattened calf and kill it, and let
us eat and celebrate. For this my son [daughter]
was dead, and is alive again; he [she] was lost,
and is found." And they began to celebrate."
—Luke 15:21–24, The Bible

———

Steve and I were engaged by Christmastime. I don't remember a proposal. It seemed like the obvious and natural path. He was the kindest, gentlest man I had ever met. The fact that he drank bourbon and smoked Salem menthols seemed irrelevant. In fact, I soon adopted both of those vices as well. I had fallen a long way from the smug, self-righteous Mennonite girl of just a few years back.

After mostly choosing not to attend and thereby flunking all of my fall classes except choir, I left Bethel College and got a job as a receptionist for a large paper company. Steve finished his undergraduate degree in fine arts and worked at a tree nursery. Our aim was to make enough money to return to Paraguay together. To get married.

•••

It was cold and cloudy that winter day in June of 1971 when Steve and I landed in Asunción. I was twenty and my soon-to-be husband was twenty-seven. My brother Wesley met us at the airport in his beat-up Mitsubishi and took us to the leprosy station at Km. 81. Steve sat in the front passenger seat next to Wesley, back straight, staring wide-eyed at the countryside we were passing.

"Ah, this air," he said, inhaling deeply. "This air smells just like India." He turned to me in the back seat and smiled. "But this is definitely not India, not nearly enough people."

Wesley glanced over at him. "What do you mean, not enough people?"

"Well, where I'm from in northern India, the masses of people are almost overwhelming. This seems so much less populated. But the rest of it sure feels like I'm home."

From the back, I could see the satisfied smile on Steve's face. I sat back against the seat, closed my eyes, and allowed the pungent, smoky Paraguay air from the open window to blow across my body.

Going back to Paraguay to get married had seemed as inevitable as marrying Steve. I had missed my home and still felt like a stranger in a strange land in the US. The forces pulling me back to Paraguay were as strong as the forces that had propelled me to leave only eight months earlier. The confused clash of emotions I had felt as the Braniff flight wrenched me from the red-tiled roofs of Asunción still churned within me, but with one important difference. I had been a lost young girl, needing to get away from parents whom I continuously disappointed, away from a Mennonite church that had sanctioned me and yet somehow retained a hold over me, and away from the mess I had made with a much older married man. And now here I was, returning with a man whose deep baritone voice resonated in my whole being. The man who promised to always love me in the morning.

Wesley made the turn at the Km. 81 marker, the entrance to the leprosy station. I saw the curves of the deeply rutted dirt road that I knew so well, winding its way the two and a half kilometers up the hill to the station. We approached our L-shaped red brick house at about suppertime. I saw the familiar purple bougainvillea arch at the entryway, the wide-bladed grass, mom's rosebushes and the open veranda.

I jumped out of the car before it came to a full stop.

"Marlena!" My little brother Cresencio had spilled milk all over his shirt in his excitement. He rushed into my arms.

I saw my folks and my two younger sisters appear from the veranda. I couldn't quite make out my parents' expressions. *Was it excitement? Was it unease? I had written them about this man, especially emphasizing the missionary-son part, but what would they think of him?* Suddenly a bit unsure of myself, I turned back to take hold of Steve's hand.

"Dad, Mom." My voice cracked. "I... I want you to meet the man I want to marry. This is Steve."

Mom came forward first, holding her arms out to hug me. "I hope this is God's will for you," she said softly.

"Dad, it's good to be home." I pulled away from my mother and reached toward him.

"Marlena," he said hoarsely, hugging me.

My mother turned to Steve.

"Welcome, Steve," she said, her voice warm, but her body rigid with tension as she reached to give him a hug.

Hands still resting on Mom's shoulders, Steve looked her steadily in the eyes. "It's so good for me to be here, to finally meet you. I love your daughter very much and being here to get to know you, her parents, and to get married here means a lot to me." He paused and grinned. "And Paraguay feels just like home."

Mom expelled air from her lungs as though she had been holding her breath, and her shoulders slowly dropped from her ears.

"And you're a good Christian son of missionaries in India?" Her voice rose at the end, turning what began as a statement into a question.

"Yes, my parents are Presbyterian missionaries in Kanpur, India," Steve said, expertly evading a direct answer to the question about whether or not he was a "good Christian."

"*Najo*," Dad said, turning to Steve and reaching out a hand. "So you're Steve."

I had warned Steve that my father was not a warm and fuzzy kind of guy. But Steve nonetheless seemed at a loss for words in response to Dad's greeting.

"Let's get our bags out of the car," I said quickly.

Mom started toward my brother's car.

"I won't let my wonderful soon-to-be-mother-in-law carry those heavy bags," Steve said, casually putting an arm around her shoulder.

Mom smiled at him, and I could have sworn I saw a twinkle in her eyes.

"Marlena, you know where the girls' room is," my mother said. "Steve, I'll show you the room we fixed up just for you."

•••

We had arrived less than a week before the wedding, which we planned to hold in my childhood home with just my family and a few close friends. On the day of the wedding, Saturday, June 26, my brother Wesley drove us to Asunción with a VW pickup (a leprosy station vehicle) to do last-minute shopping and get back in time to fix up the house for the marriage ceremony later that day.

We made it back to the leprosy station by four thirty. An hour later, we had arranged three dozen red roses into vases and placed them on the red brick fireplace and elsewhere around the living room. And we had assembled sixteen corsages with little white carnations for each of the guests. The lighting consisted of a few dozen white candles that we had set up around the living room.

It was time to shower and get dressed for the big event. I pulled out the traditional Indian wedding sari that Steve's parents had sent us. It was deep red with real gold embroidery. I hadn't met his folks since they lived in India and I hardly knew them at all, but they seemed very accepting of me and of our marriage. I thought about how excited I had been when they asked whether I would wear an Indian sari for our wedding. And relieved. It allowed me to avoid the embarrassment of facing my parents' questions about whether I should be allowed to wear a traditional white wedding gown and veil, given that I wasn't a virgin.

I tied the sari and combed my hair alone in my parents' bedroom, lit

Nothing Bad Between Us

by a kerosene lamp. As my eyes met their reflection in my mother's smoky cracked mirror, I smiled. The dark eyes shining back at me were glistening with promise: *You will never again be alone. You will never again be an unwanted extra person in someone else's home. And he will always love you in the morning.*

The minister we had chosen was a friend of my folks. The main criterion for choosing him was his fluency in both German and English, since the ceremony was to consist of both. When everyone had pinned on their corsages and people were seated in the living room, Steve came to get me from my folks' room and we casually walked together into the living room.

We had asked Mom to say a few words in English. "When Marlena left for the States a year ago, we were concerned about where she would find her place in life... We believe the Lord has led you two together, and we are very thankful..."

After a few German hymns, we very informally spoke our vows and the minister married us. Dad closed the ceremony with a long prayer of thanksgiving, spoken partly in German and partly in English.

Steve turned to my mother. "Mom, whatever you have been cooking all day for our wedding feast smells absolutely delicious. Are we ready to eat?"

"We are," she said, putting her arm around his waist. "We have tomato and lettuce salad, roasted duck and rooster, mashed potatoes, carrots, and peas, and Coca Cola to drink. And..." Mom paused, her eyes smiling at Steve. "I made fresh homemade rolls especially for you."

"I must be your favorite son-in-law." They both laughed.

After the wedding dinner, people began drifting toward bed. Steve and I remained at the table, quietly holding hands, not ready for the evening to end. Dad came over and sat down next to us. He cleared his throat, his eyes on the floor.

"What is it, Dad?" Steve asked.

Dad cleared his throat again. "*Najo*, I need to talk to you both about something. I'm afraid it's not a very happy subject."

"What's the matter?" I asked, hoping this unhappy subject wasn't about to ruin the best night of my life.

"I just need to remind you that you have only a very small chance of getting pregnant, Marlena, with the one quarter of one ovary you have left," he said. "If you want to have a baby, I would recommend that you try right away. Your chances will most likely go down over time." He rose to leave, then turned back toward us. "May the good Lord richly bless your union."

We were both well aware of the sad truth about my partial ovary. But Dad's words were sobering nonetheless.

"Let's make a baby," Steve whispered in my ear, leading me to his bedroom.

•••

A few weeks after our wedding, the folks asked to speak with us. The four of us were sitting in front of the fireplace in our living room, our hands stretched toward the roaring fire.

"Can I get you some tea, Steve?" Mom asked.

"Thanks, no, Mom, I'm fine. Can I get you anything?" Steve said. I watched the two of them and smiled.

"So, we wanted to talk with you two about some plans we're making," Dad said. We both turned toward him. He sounded so serious. "For some time now I've been reading the American Medical Association's calls for medical personnel in Vietnam, where the war's still raging and leprosy continues to be a big problem. Well, Mom and I feel called to serve there."

"For how long?" Steve asked.

"If we spend four months in Vietnam, the AMA will give us two around-the-world tickets with as many stops as we want. This means we could then also make some stops in India, Germany, and Israel, all places we've wanted to go. We'd also be able to attend the Christian Hospital Fellowship conference in Austria. The whole travel circuit we are imagining would take about a year and a half."

"What about the leprosy work here?" I asked.

My folks looked at each other, and for a moment neither of them spoke.

"Well, Daddy has not been happy about the Mennonite colony leadership and MCC telling him how to run the station differently. After Daddy poured his life into creating and running one of the most effective treatment centers for leprosy in the world, they now say they can't tolerate his autocratic ways. Some wrong ideas have been spread in the Chaco Mennonite colonies..." My mother's voice trailed off.

"What wrong ideas?" I was leaning forward.

"Let's not get into all that, Clara," Dad said, pausing to add wood to the fire. "The point is that we will not be returning here to the leprosy station after the Vietnam service tour."

I stared at my father, my eyes open wide with questions. After twenty years of devoted service, after my whole life of him leading the leprosy work at Km. 81, it was impossible for me to even imagine Dad without it.

He continued. "Our thought is that after we return, we'd like to move to east Paraguay, near the Brazilian border, and set up a small rural clinic in an area that has no doctor."

"We've been praying a lot about this," Mom said. "We don't know who might take care of Josefina and Cresencio (my adopted sister and brother, then eight and ten) for the year and a half that we would be gone. And we also need to find someone to oversee the construction of our new house out in east Paraguay. Dad has already drawn up the plans for the house."

"You've already drawn up plans for the house?" I shook my head. "You've been planning this for a while now?"

"Well, we're praying to learn what God's plan is for us now that we're done with the leprosy work." Dad's back was bent over and his face was drawn. For the first time, I noticed how much older he looked than his sixty years. It scared me to think that maybe he wasn't completely invincible.

I sat back and stared into the fire. As was the case with so many aspects of my father's life, he was saying very little about this seemingly premature departure from leprosy work. But it looked like a huge deal to me, and instead of rejoicing that the leprosy station, my greatest rival for my dad's attention, was falling away, I felt sad and confused. We learned much later that the very leadership traits that had allowed the leprosy work to be born and to initially flourish (strict control, autocratic decision-making, and a singular vision) had become traits that got in the way of the station's continued expansion.

In our bedroom later that evening, Steve turned to me. "I don't really know what we're going to do after going back to the States. Do you think maybe we should consider staying and...?"

I interrupted him. "Are you saying you think we should stay here and build a house and take care of two kids for a year and a half? We know nothing about building houses, Steve, and you have no idea how hard that would be, given that nothing works efficiently in this country. And besides..." My voice trailed off. There weren't many good arguments not to do this. We had come to Paraguay with one-way tickets, not knowing how long we would stay or what we would do upon our return to the States. I had earned no college credits, except for the one credit hour for choir. He had a bachelor's degree in music and a God-given great voice, neither of which would easily provide a roof over our heads or food on our table. We had no money, little earning power, and no plans for our lives.

Leaving Paraguay the year before had felt like an escape from misery. But it also had felt like I was being torn from my roots. This evening, lying next to my new husband and scheming about this possible adventure together, I realized that Paraguay and all of its tribes, the Chaco colonies, the Mennonite church and my family, were like a formidable magnet, pulling me back in despite all of my reasons never to return. And the vulnerable cracks in my father's strong armor that I had witnessed for the first time earlier that evening led me to want, somehow, to reach out and help.

"We could make this a year of focusing on making our baby, too," Steve said, pulling me toward him.

So, this time, Steve and I became the instruments of "God will Provide" for my folks. We offered to stay in Paraguay for that year and a half, take care of the two children, and oversee the construction of their house.

•••

We moved into a little two-room shack near the spot where the new house was to be built. We had a well, a *Klo* (outhouse), and an outdoor woodburning cooking stove. We brought beds and essential kitchenware from the house at Km. 81. We bought half dozen chickens that provided a paltry number of eggs. And we acquired a cow, Molly, who provided milk, cream, and butter. Since we had no electricity for a fridge, we milked our Molly every day to get

Nothing Bad Between Us

just the amount of milk we needed for that day.

When we agreed to take on the project, we had in mind that we would be overseeing the construction of the house. We soon learned that constant hands-on involvement was the only way to keep things moving. We knew nothing about construction. Dad had drawn the architectural plans for the house himself. They were often confusing and vague. Steve spoke no German and no Spanish, so the only way for him to communicate with German Mennonite or Paraguayan construction workers was through me as an interpreter. My little brother and sister were great, but instant parenting was hardly something we were prepared for.

•••

Steve and I had begun trying to make a baby the night of our wedding. Every month, we would grieve when my period came, shattering our hopes, which were shaky to begin with, given what Dad had told us about the declining usefulness of my quarter of an ovary.

But in December, just six months later, tests at the *Hospital Bautista* in Asunción confirmed it.

"We're going to have our baby at the beginning of September!" Steve threw his arms around me, then crouched down and gently placed his face against my belly. "It'll be a girl," he said.

I nodded, thinking about how Dad had ordered me, his dark-eyed girl.

"September. The folks will be back by then. How do you feel about Dad delivering our girl?" I looked over at Steve, expecting him to want us to return to the States to have the baby in a regular hospital.

For me the idea that my father would deliver our baby followed naturally from the way I had grown up. Dad had surgically removed my tonsils, had given us kids disgusting medication to rid us of hookworms, had given us rabies shots in the belly, and had dug pinworms out of all of our butts. But this might be different for Steve. This was our miracle baby.

"I think that's a great idea," Steve said.

We sent the folks a letter giving them our news and asking if they would deliver the baby.

We know that this miracle baby would not have been possible if you had not asked Dr. McDowell to save a part of my left ovary, Dad, I wrote. *We would be honored if you would consider delivering the child.*

It took six weeks for us to hear back from the folks. I waved the letter in the air in front of me as I ran into our shack.

"Look Steve, it's from the folks. I'll bet they are so, so excited!"

I ripped open the letter. It was in my mother's handwriting. I scanned down the first page, seeing only newsy items about their travels. At the top of the second page, I read, *It's very good news that you are pregnant. And of course, Daddy and I would be pleased to deliver the baby in September.* Then she went on to describe the missionaries they had visited the prior week.

Steve saw the tears starting to well up in my eyes and reached out to hug me. "They must just be very preoccupied right now," he murmured in my ear.

•••

They had been gone for a year and a half. We were almost giddy with anticipation the evening they were scheduled to return to their new house in east Paraguay. Steve and I had worked twelve-hour days for the past several weeks to get the ceilings and floors of the house sanded and varnished and to get all of the million details finished. My back ached and my swollen feet and legs begged for mercy, but we were determined to get everything done before they returned.

Just in time, the house was finished down to every last detail. A pot of *Borscht* (Russian Mennonite cabbage soup) was on the stove. A fire blazed in the huge stone fireplace we had designed and built, rock by rock. The two children and Steve and I sat on cushions in front of the fire. We waited. And waited.

"What time is it?" I mumbled as I came out of a deep sleep, wrapping a blanket around my considerable seven-months-pregnant bulk. The fire was long out. My adopted brother and sister, Cresencio and Josefina, were lying across our laps, sound asleep.

Steve gently pushed the children off and rose to find a flashlight. "It's past two in the morning." He groaned. "And I'm cold. Let's get these kids to

Nothing Bad Between Us

bed and get under some blankets ourselves."

The folks arrived late that morning. There was no fire, the *Borscht* seemed irrelevant, and we felt stiff and cranky.

My brother and sister ran out of the house to greet them. Steve and I followed.

"Look at my belly, Mom." I took her hands in mine and placed them on either side of my swollen body. I was about to be a mother and wanted to share the magic with my own mother.

"Nice," she said, with an almost-smile. She appeared distant. Her face was blank. I barely held back the tears.

I turned to my father, who seemed to have aged a decade in the year and a half since they left. His shoulders were hunched over and his eyes were clouded.

"Welcome, home, Dad," I said.

"Home?" he asked under his breath, as I hugged him.

"Come see the house," Steve said, grabbing two of their suitcases and leading the way. We held our breath as they entered and looked around.

"Nice," Mom said again as they walked from room to room. Dad said nothing.

Steve pulled me aside. "What's the deal here?" he asked. "Did we just bust our buns to get this house built for him and he says nothing?"

"I know, Steve," I whispered back. "It feels like he really doesn't care about this or about anything else, for that matter."

We moved toward the kitchen.

"Why did you build that planter over by the breakfast bar? How much did that cost?" Dad frowned. His voice sounded gruff.

I looked toward my mother, silently willing her to say how much she loved it. The planter had not been part of Dad's drawings. Steve and I had added it as a special surprise for Mom. I had even found a philodendron plant, which was already beginning to climb up the wrought iron trellis.

But Mom said nothing, just looked at my father with hooded eyes.

Steve backed up and grabbed my hand. "Shit," he whispered under his breath. "Let's get out of here."

In our little two-room shack that afternoon, while the folks were "resting" in their bedroom, Steve and I came up with a plan to get out, to take a break from it all. We would spend the next three weeks in Argentina and Uruguay, traveling on buses and trains.

The following morning at breakfast, we told the folks about our plan. "We just need to take a little break," I said, staring into my coffee cup. I was afraid they would be terribly sad and disappointed that we were leaving so soon after their arrival.

"Oh, that's nice," Mom said, with that almost-smile pasted on her face. *Had they even heard what we told them?* They both seemed enveloped in an impenetrable fog.

●●●

When we returned to east Paraguay three weeks later, it was almost time for me to deliver our baby. Steve and I knew it would be a girl. We had named her Shareen, which Steve said in Hindi meant "very sweet."

My water broke at around eight in the evening on September 14.

"Steve, I need to pee. Can you come outside with me?" I asked.

It was a starless, moonless, cloudy night. He led me down the dirt path to our *Klo*.

"No, not there. I can't pee in the *Klo*." I shrank back.

"Why not?" he asked.

"Our baby might pop out and land in that black stinking swamp of poop and maggots." Even during normal times, when I wasn't about to deliver a baby, I had a hard time using the *Klo* at night, scared that snakes would come up from below and snap at my butt.

I peed in the grass outside of our little shack. If she came out there, the landing would be soft, I figured.

●●●

Around midnight, with considerable trepidation, Steve walked past the pump house and across the yard the short distance to Mom and Dad's new house to let them know that the contractions were becoming more regular and more frequent.

He knocked softly on the folks' bedroom door. "I think it's time, Dad," he said apprehensively.

They made their way to our shack. I lay naked under a sheet. I had rolled my swollen body off to one side of the bed and was gripping the thin mattress with both hands as contractions ripped through my belly.

My father pushed the sheet aside. "Bring your knees up...like this," he said. "I need to see what's going on."

"OK, you're dilating nicely. But it'll still be a while."

"Please stay with me." I gasped as I felt the throbbing begin again.

Between contractions, I looked around the dim lamplit room and smiled. I saw Steve with his camera, recording this miracle of ours. And both of my parents stooped over my bed, attending to me, their fog lifted, at least for now.

At eight o'clock the next morning, my father held Shareen in his bare hand, as he had held me twenty-one years earlier.

Ever so gently, he laid the baby on my chest. He placed his hand, still bloodied from the delivery, on my forehead and said quietly, "Well done, Marlena."

CHAPTER 10:
Safe and Numb (1972–1975)

Who am I?

———

"The days hardened with cold and boredom
like last year's loaves of bread. One began
to cut them with blunt knives without
appetite, with a lazy indifference."

—Bruno Schulz, *The Street of Crocodiles*

———

Shareen was the miracle we had wished for. After a few weeks of colic, she hardly ever cried. And when she smiled, her big blue eyes sparkled. It seemed like she and the universe had made a pact that joy was to be her lot in life. We called her our *Little Sunshine*. I held my girl close to my heart, sang to her, and whispered in her ear about always being there for her and never, ever leaving her alone.

When Shareen was three weeks old, the three of us returned to Kansas, not knowing what lay ahead. There weren't many job opportunities for a baritone wannabe opera singer with a bachelor's degree, or for me with no degree at all and a baby girl.

"You can get a master's degree at Wichita State," I suggested. "That way you can teach music just in case you don't get to sing opera the way you want."

"I can't do that," he said. "What would we live on?"

"I'll find a job as a waitress. I can work nights when you're at home with Shareen," I said, confident that we would find a way.

The master's program at WSU was a good fit for Steve. He spent his days on campus. And I worked late into the night, serving drinks in the bar at a Steak and Ale restaurant.

Sometimes when I was alone, driving to or from the restaurant, I thought about how my life had turned out. *Who was I*, I wondered, *besides a devoted mom*? I had no dreams for myself, no aspirations, no goals, other than to work hard enough so we could one day move to New York City so Steve could sing opera in the big leagues.

But it's OK, I told myself. I knew I could rest in the assurance that Steve would always be there to "love me in the morning."

•••

I was running late for work. I slammed the gas pedal of our light blue, beat-up VW bug to the floor, but it only shuddered in response, maintaining its slow forward motion. I glanced in the rearview mirror, frowned, and pushed back a strand of the unruly hair that I had forgotten to comb properly before rushing out of the house.

"Phone me at the restaurant if she gets any worse?" I had called out to Steve before leaving.

Shareen, not even a year old, had a high fever. She had been getting those recently. I made up my mind to take her to a doctor the next day. We'd figure out some way to pay for it.

I pulled into the Steak and Ale parking lot, parked the car, and ran in through the back door.

"Hey there. You're late." The night manager scowled. "Al over there by the bar has been asking for you."

"Peter, please, I've told you about that man. Three times he has groped my behind, and last week when he got especially drunk, he tried to fondle my breasts."

Peter ogled my legs under the short red skirt that was part of the Steak and Ale uniform. Then he raised his eyes to take in the rise of my breasts under the low-cut neckline of the white Dirndl-type German peasant blouse. "Well, you do look mighty tempting in that little outfit," he said.

I wish we didn't need the money, I thought to myself. *I wish I could just leave. I want to be with my girl.* Aloud I said, "I've clocked in," and headed for the bar.

•••

My job at Steak and Ale and Steve's VA check were our only sources of income. So we could barely afford to rent a very small ranch-style house on the east side of Wichita. Indian batiks lined the living room walls. On the floor were four huge pillows I had sewn, stuffed with ripped-up pieces of a foam mattress from the Salvation Army. Three pots of spider plants hung from the ceiling in macramé plant hangers. Half a dozen rhododendrons snaked their way nearly to the ceiling along wooden trellises Steve had built.

He and I stood in the middle of our living room, wondering what my folks would think of our home. They were in the States for a visit and were coming to see us for the first time.

"When are they going to get here?" Steve asked uneasily, eyeing the numerous butt-filled ashtrays around the house. "We need to get this house aired out."

"I'm not sure when they were planning on leaving Uncle Herman's house (just east of Newton), but I think they'll be here sometime this afternoon," I said.

"You empty the ashtrays and stash them somewhere. I'll open all the windows," I said.

A bitter wind swept through the house. It was a snowy, ten-degree Kansas winter day.

"What should I do with these?" Steve asked. He pulled a six-pack of beer from the back of the fridge.

"Isn't there room under the workbench in the garage? That's where I hid the bourbon," I said.

Steve and I had quit smoking and drinking during the time we were in Paraguay, but started up again when we returned to the States. When either set of parents came to visit, we would hide the cigarettes and alcohol like naughty young children. We wanted the folks to think that we were an upstanding Christian family. As soon as they left, those lovely addictions behind which we hid came out of their hiding places under the workbench in our garage and at the bottom of our bedroom closet. It occurs to me now that we were perfectly reenacting the pattern of presenting a façade of the "happy, happy family," which had been my family's pattern all my life. My parents were largely absent when I was a child. And our times together were often filled with rage, especially between my dad and me. But to the outside world we presented an image of a close-knit Christian family. I knew the happy-family formula well.

"They're here!" I saw my Uncle Herman's station wagon pull into our driveway, and my breath caught in my throat as I watched my parents get out of the car. My father's back was as straight as ever, but there was something about the way he held his head, bent over, that made him seem to me much older than sixty-two. They both looked like they were drowning in old tattered coats several sizes too large for them. I suspected the coats had come from Etcetera, a thrift store in Newton, one of a chain of such shops that produced income for the programs of the Mennonite Central Committee, including the leprosy work my parents had founded in Paraguay.

I glanced anxiously at Steve and knew that he too was remembering the tensions in Paraguay the last time we saw them, around the time Shareen was born. But the folks' letters to us over the past year and a half had been full of praise and appreciation for the work we did on their house. I took Steve's hand in mine. It was going to be all right.

"Mom, Dad, welcome to our home," I said, grabbing one of their bags.

"Oh my, it is so good to be here, to finally see your place," my mother said, looking around.

"Sorry it's a bit chilly. We have the heat going, and it'll be warmer soon," Steve said, rubbing his cold hands together. We had closed the windows back up just moments before the folks arrived.

"Oh, it's just fine like it is," Dad said. "I'm pleased you're not *veschwenderisch*—wasteful, spending lots of money to heat up your house to make it feel like it's summertime."

"Where's our little Shareen?" Mom asked.

"She's still taking her nap, but come, let's go wake her up," I said, leading my mother to our daughter's room.

"You have a very nice home here," I heard my father say as we walked toward Shareen's bedroom.

"Shareen, your *Grossma*'s here," I said softly.

Mom reached into Shareen's crib and gently patted her back. "She's so beautiful, Marlena," she said, her warm eyes turning from the crib to me.

•••

Shareen was taking her first baby steps.

"She's so advanced, walking so soon," Steve said, grinning at our daughter.

"Yes, she is," I said. "But I'm worried that her feet turn in when she walks. Do you think we should see a doctor about that?"

"I'm sure she'll outgrow that," Steve said.

But after a few months, she hadn't outgrown it. I made an appointment with a podiatrist. I had never even heard of a podiatrist before.

"OK, let's see her walk across the room," the doctor said after I explained why we were there. He was a short, Asian man in a very long white coat.

Shareen obediently tottered across the small office, her big toes pointing in toward each other.

"Hmmm, in-toeing is usually nothing to worry about for a toddler. But this is a bit more severe than I would like to see," he said, rubbing his chin. "I think I will prescribe a brace for her feet that she'll have to wear every night until we get the lower leg bone to tilt outward a bit."

He scribbled something on his notepad. "Here's the address. That's where you can get your daughter fitted with braces," he said, turning to leave.

"Wait. Can you tell me a little about these braces? Will they hurt her feet? How long will she need to wear them?"

"I have specified all that." He pointed to the piece of paper he had handed me. "It'll all be in the instructions when you get the braces. Come see me again in four months. We'll determine if there's been any progress."

I scooped my girl into my arms. "I won't let the braces hurt you," I murmured into her ear.

She put her arms around my neck, looked up at me with her big blue eyes, and smiled.

There were moments, like this one, when all of the love and caring I had ever felt became distilled and poured into that one small child, my miracle baby.

•••

The three of us fell into a quiet routine. Up by eight o'clock. Steve at school. Shareen playing in the backyard with the neighbor kids. Going to the park. Cooking supper. Steve back. Serving drunk guys in the bar at Steak and Ale. Crawling soundlessly into bed after midnight so as not to awaken Steve. Exhausted. Up again by eight o'clock.

I watched my body go through the motions of caretaking and waitressing as though I no longer inhabited it. It was just doing what was needed on automatic. I felt cut off from it, disconnected. My heart lay down and went to sleep, even though I continued, on the outside, to look like an ordinary waitress, or wife, or mother, or whatever role I was playing out at that moment.

Sometimes late at night, my feet still stinging from the long shift at the bar, I sat at the edge of our bed and looked at my sleeping husband. My mind wandered to the day we met just weeks after my arrival in the States. To the warmth and safety of his embrace. Steve was a good man, always ready with a smile or a joke to brighten the moment. And yet...like Matthew Arnold said in a poem I loved, "A Buried Life," my husband's light words and gay smiles didn't reach the places deep within me that longed to be touched.

What happened to us? I mouthed the words silently. *Do you even know who I am? Do I?*

Nothing Bad Between Us

We had been in Wichita for two years when something happened that we were sure would give Steve the break he needed to make it big in the world of opera.

"Look what came." Steve grinned. He was sitting at the kitchen table, sorting through a stack of mail that had accumulated. "It's a letter from the Kansas Patronage of the Arts."

I held my breath and sat down beside him. My Uncle Herb's wife, Mariam, was an influential member of and contributor to the patronage organization. She had told us that she would try to pull some strings to see if the organization might fund a trip for Steve to spend two months in Aachen, Germany, to sing in the opera house there. It would surely open doors for a successful career as an opera singer.

He ripped open the envelope and began to read. "Dear Mr. Fiol. We are pleased to inform you that you have been chosen..."

I jumped from my chair. "Steve, this is it! It's the chance we've been waiting for."

Six weeks later, Steve was on his way to the big time. Our neighbor agreed to keep Shareen at her house while I was at work. It was a time of huge optimism for us.

But the letters from him sounded increasingly gloomy. *I'm not getting any good roles, and I'm certainly not getting any leads for the future. I'm beginning to think this was a waste of my time*, he wrote after being there for just three weeks.

I wrote back encouraging letters about sticking with it. Something good had to come of this amazing break we had gotten.

And then my world collapsed.

Shareen, then two and a half, had developed one of those high fevers that she was prone to get. I had given her lots of liquids and baby aspirin and I had kept a cold wet washcloth on her forehead. But the fever wouldn't come down.

My hand shook as I put the rectal thermometer into her anus for the sixth time that night. It read 104!

"Oh, my Sweet Sunshine," I cried. "Oh, my baby. I can't get this fever down. We have to go to the emergency room."

I glanced at the clock. It was past midnight, too late to ask my neighbor to come with me. I wrapped my sick girl in a blanket. As I laid her on the back seat of the VW bug, I saw her eyes roll back into her head.

"Please, baby girl, please hang on. I'm getting you to the hospital." I repeated those words, like a mantra, all the way to Wesley Medical Center.

The attending physician took one look at her and sent her immediately to the ICU. My child lay inside an ice tent for two days while the doctors poked and prodded and tested specimens to try to determine the cause of the fever. She looked so tiny and so helpless, lying there in that bed inside a clear plastic tent with ice packs all around her small body.

I parked myself beside her tent and refused to leave. When she was awake, I sang all of her favorite songs, over and over. *The itsy-bitsy spider crawled up the waterspout* and *M-I-C-K-E-Y-M-O-U-S-E*. When she slept, I tried to pray to a God I had rejected for years. *Please, dear God. Please make my girl get well. If you're really up there, please hear my prayer.*

Every nerve in my body had come alive. I felt an edge, a fervor that I hardly recognized. It had been a long time since anything had pierced the thick curtain of numbness that had become my day-to-day married life.

The breakthrough came on the third day, when the doctors finally discovered that she had a condition called urinary reflux, the backward flow of urine from the bladder into the kidneys. They put her on antibiotics and sent us home.

"Come back in two weeks and we'll see how the antibiotics are working," the urologist said, as he signed the papers for her release.

I wrote Steve a letter, telling him what had happened and that Shareen was now OK. She seemed much better when we went back to the doctor a few weeks later.

"Mrs. Fiol, we recommend an anti-reflux procedure that will prevent the flow of urine from the bladder back up the tubes," the urologist said. "The antibiotics alone are not doing the job."

During the procedure the following week, I held my baby's little head in my arms, as she lay on the examining table, writhing and screaming in pain. Her cries tore through me. The new edge of aliveness I had begun to experience over the past few weeks rose to a peak. I faced the doctor and said,

"You're never doing this to her again, ever, unless you give her something to make it less painful."

He looked at me and frowned, pulling the gloves from his hands.

By the time Steve returned from Germany, things returned to normal: Shareen's health. Even Steve's lack of job options. Germany hadn't generated any prospects for an opera career. We returned to our quiet day-to-day routine.

•••

"We got a letter from your folks," Steve said one sunny, hot afternoon when I walked into the house, holding a grocery bag in one arm and balancing Shareen on my other hip. "It's on the table."

It had been three years since we had left the folks after building their new house in east Paraguay and over a year since they had visited us in Kansas. I knew from prior letters that life in east Paraguay was not all they had hoped. But it took weeks for letters to go back and forth, so I was eager to hear the latest.

I set the grocery bag on the kitchen table, handed Shareen a snack, and ripped open the light blue airmail envelope.

We don't feel very valuable here, I read my mother's words out loud to Steve. *There are very few patients who even know that we are here. And often, when they do come, we can't perform the surgery or the procedure that they need.* She shared news about some of their neighbors we still knew from our time there. She ended her part of the letter with *It's just so hard for me to see Daddy so dejected and feeling so useless.*

Then my father's clipped sentences in his loopy, bold handwriting began. *Our dear ones in Kansas. Saw a patient today who had a large knot in his abdomen. High fever. Probably not long to live. But I don't have the facility here to cut him open. So I had to send him to Coronel Oviedo. I'm not sure I know what we're doing here now.*

I looked up from the letter, tears stinging my eyes.

"Dad's whole life has always been about being somehow beyond ordinary. Ever since I can remember, he was a man driven to never be just average. I can't even imagine how hard this must be for him," I said.

Steve came around to where I was standing and put his arm around my shoulder. "I can now better understand why they were so depressed when they returned from Vietnam to the new house we built them in east Paraguay. Leaving the leprosy station and then simply becoming a good doctor in a small, unknown country clinic out in the backwoods of east Paraguay must have left him feeling just ordinary and no longer important like he used to be." He paused and then concluded. "The eyes of the world are no longer on him and his work."

I closed my eyes and thought about the crazy man who had taken his new bride to the land where "no white man can live." The man who performed surgeries he had never seen done, with no textbooks to guide him. The man who ventured out alone across the Paraguayan backcountry on horseback to find leprosy patients. Who revolutionized the treatment of leprosy around the world. "I just feel so sad and so helpless to do anything for them," I said, sagging against my husband.

"The great part about their letters is how much they love and trust us. How much they confide in us, even about the stuff that's not going so well," he said, always the one to look for the silver lining.

I smiled through my tears. "Well, yes, marrying you made me legitimate in their eyes. I went from being the sick child they hardly knew what to do with to someone they actually seem to like and even respect."

•••

Steve and Shareen were usually sound asleep when I got home from my evening shift at Steak and Ale.

One night, as I pulled our VW bug into the driveway, I noticed that our bedroom light was still on. I slid my key into the door, schlepped my sore feet into the house, and kicked off my shoes.

Steve stood in the middle of the living room, dimly lit from the light in the bedroom. He looked like he had just stepped out of the shower. His dark hair, now cut short, was combed back from his high forehead. He wore only a *lungi*, an Indian cloth tied around the waist, fastened with a double twist knot in the front.

"Steve, what are you doing up? It's late. Are you OK?" I asked.

"It's been so long," he murmured, awkwardly placing a hand on my shoulder.

"Oh..." My voice faltered. He was right. It had been a long time. And I hadn't even thought about it. I felt the weight of my guilt pressing down on me.

Steve led me into our bedroom and closed the door. Gently he pulled me toward him.

I closed my eyes as his weight came down on me. *This is so sad. We don't even pretend to be passionate anymore,* I thought.

After, I lay wide-awake beside him, listening to his deep and regular breathing. I inched my hand toward him and placed just one finger lightly against his hip. A single tear made its way down my cheek, then another.

How did our love become so flat? I wondered. *When did we stop reaching for each other with fire in our eyes and butterflies in our stomach? Did all marriages inevitably end up like this?* A small sob rose in my throat.

Steve stirred and then awakened. When he saw that I wasn't asleep he sat up. "Are you alright? Do you need me to get you anything?"

"No, I'm fine, honey. Go back to sleep," I said, kissing him lightly on the forehead.

CHAPTER 11:
Keeping It All Together (1975–1980)

Our family in 1978

———

"Her eyes were full of a hot liquid...which, without
disturbing the firmness of her lips, made the air
thick, rolled down her cheeks. She had perfect
control of herself—Oh, yes!—in every other way."

—Virginia Woolf, *To the Lighthouse*

———

Steve and I wanted a sibling for our Shareen. But we didn't want to add to the population explosion, so we opted for adoption.

"I'm so sorry to give you this news," said the lady sitting primly behind her metal desk at the adoption agency. She looked at us over the concave, rimless-at-the-top reading glasses that rested at the end of her small, sharp nose. The glasses were attached to silver chains that hung down on either side of her face.

"But..." My voice broke and I looked over at Steve. "We..."

Steve leaned forward in his chair. "We have a home, we have a three-year-old daughter who is always well fed and clothed. We are attentive and loving parents. What more could you ask for?" His voice held an edge I didn't often hear.

"You do not make the financial cut," she said, firmly closing the notebook on her desk. "Your income is insufficient for us to consider you as adoptive parents." She rose, indicating it was time for us to leave.

As we walked to our car, I reached for Steve's hand. "She just told us we're not fit to be parents," I said. "It's the one thing I thought I could do really well." A hard lump was forming in my throat.

"You *do* do it really well," he said. After a pause, he added, "If they're not going to let us adopt, how about we make another baby ourselves?"

"But we weren't going to contribute to the *Population Bomb*?" I said, my voice rising at the end to form a question, emphasizing the last two words.

We drove home in silence.

Like so many others in the US in the 1970s, we had read Paul Ehrlich's 1968 book *The Population Bomb*. He predicted that humankind stood on the brink of apocalypse because there were too many of us. Hundreds of millions would starve to death in the 1970s. Steve and I took this very seriously. We didn't want to be a part of the cause of that catastrophe. But we had been denied the option to adopt.

•••

By the time our son Stefan was born a little over a year later, Steve had landed a teaching position at Millikin, a small college in central Illinois.

"You could take some classes at Millikin. My schedule is flexible. I can watch the kids while you're in class," he offered.

"I can't, Steve. I'm still nursing the baby. And I'm so worried about Shareen's stuttering." I lowered my voice so our daughter wouldn't hear me. "I read the other day that it may be a symptom of psychological problems when a child starts stuttering like that. I feel like I need to give her more time, so she doesn't think her baby brother's taken us away from her."

"I'll help you with that," he said. "We're in this together, remember?" He put an arm around my shoulders, and I leaned into him.

"OK, I'll get a class schedule. Maybe it could work," I said.

We were in it together, as he said, and we synchronized perfectly. Three mornings a week, Steve drove home from his office in our brand-new brown

Pinto station wagon to spend two hours with the children while I attended class at Millikin. I came directly home after class, just in time for him to hurry back to work.

One evening, after the kids were fed, bathed, had stories read to them, and were tucked into bed, Steve asked. "What do you think about me auditioning to sing at the Muny Theater in St. Louis this summer?"

"Is that what you want to do?" I asked, looking up from *Madame Bovary*, which I needed to review for my French literature class the following day.

"I think I do. But it would mean that I'd have to live in St. Louis for most of the summer. You'd be alone with the kids for a few months. The season runs from mid-June to mid-August."

"You should audition," I said, knowing how much this would mean to him. "The kids and I can get along. And besides, we could drive down to see you once in a while. St. Louis isn't that far away."

My husband's deep baritone voice performed in Broadway-style musicals at the Muny in St. Louis that summer and for several summers after that.

•••

"You are so lucky to have such a great husband and family." Emily, the wife of one of Steve's colleagues, was giving me a ride home after a class.

"You mean because Steve cooks and cleans and helps me with the kids?" I asked. She had just shared with me that her husband did none of these things.

"Well, yeah. And you two always seem like you fit so perfectly together," she said, sighing. "You never fight, do you?"

"Well, I can get pretty crazed sometimes, but Steve has a real knack for diffusing any tensions that come up. He doesn't like conflict, so we really don't have any."

As I got out of Emily's car and walked toward our front door, I thought about what I had just said. It was true. We didn't fight. Steve was a good man and we had two beautiful children. There was no reason for me to feel so empty.

But I did.

•••

The phone rang and I jumped. I had been waiting for this call for hours. Last month, a scan had shown that Dad had a brain tumor and they were back in the States to have it checked out. He had been in surgery today at the Mayo Clinic, where my folks received treatment gratis as a result of their medical missionary work.

"Hi Marlena." My mother's voice sounded strained.

"Mom, tell me, what did they find?" I asked.

"The surgery lasted nine hours, Marlena," she said in a high, tight voice. "They removed a tumor the size of a little finger."

"How is he?" I asked.

"I don't know. He's still doped up in the ICU. But there's a 90 percent chance that they cut some facial nerves on his right side. That would mean that the right side of his face would be paralyzed."

"At least they were able to get the tumor out and he got through it." I exhaled deeply.

"I feel so alone here. I just wish…" My mother's voice cracked.

"I know, Mom," I said. "I wish I could be there with you, too. I feel so bad that you're going through this all by yourself."

I heard a man's voice at the other end, asking my mother to come, quick, to the ICU. "I have to go," she said. I heard the click of the phone.

I fell back onto our orange-and-brown plaid sofa and stared out of the picture window at the dirty mounds of snow in front of our house. The bleak Illinois winter landscape perfectly matched how I felt. I bent my head and put my face in both hands.

"M…mo…mo…mom…my?" Shareen leaned against me and put a hand lightly on my head.

I looked up into her questioning big blue eyes and knew that I was where I needed to be.

"It's OK, Sunshine," I said, holding her close. "Mommy's OK."

But things for my father were not OK. He spent an entire month at the Mayo Clinic, with dizziness, nausea, migraine headaches, and fainting spells. A second surgery attempted unsuccessfully to connect his tongue nerve to the severed facial nerve. The right side of his face would be permanently paralyzed, and his right ear was deaf.

Three weeks into the ordeal, my father was finally strong enough to speak over the phone.

"*Ach*, dey can yus haw my bo-y an sen wesus to We-ley," he slurred into the phone. I could barely make out the words.

"What are you saying, Dad, that you want Mayo to have your body and send the results to Wesley [my doctor brother in Paraguay]? Why would you say such a thing?" I asked.

I heard him mumble something I couldn't understand and then Mom got on the phone. "Daddy can't really talk now," she said. And then in a hushed voice, "He's very depressed, Marlena. He wants to die."

My body sagged against the wall behind me. *How could this be happening to the man who always seemed indomitable and larger than life?*

•••

In July, just six months after my father's surgeries, the folks drove from Kansas to Illinois to visit us. They oohed and aahed over cute little nine-month-old Stefan and played endless games of Candyland with Shareen. Mom tried to put on a happy face, chatting about things they were engaged in back in Kansas. After spending the month at Mayo, they had returned to Goessel, Kansas, where Dad had grown up. A new hospital in Goessel had hired him. Despite my mother's optimistic chatter, I knew from phone conversations over the course of the past few months that he had very few patients.

Dad looked haggard. His paralyzed face sagged down on the right. To keep his right eye from getting dry and irritated, he kept it covered with Saran wrap, haphazardly taped around his eye with duct tape. Even though his back was as erect as ever, he was wobbly with continued dizziness due to low blood pressure.

"Dad, I thought I'd fry you some potatoes this morning—your favorite breakfast," I said the second day they were there.

"What?" He tilted his head so that his left ear faced me. That was a gesture that would become typical of my father for the rest of his life.

"Potatoes for breakfast?" I asked, shouting into his good ear.

"*Seia gaot*—very good," he smiled a lopsided smile I still wasn't used to.

I put mugs of coffee and plates of fried potatoes, eggs, and toast on the table.

"Po...po...pot...pota..." Shareen stammered helplessly.

"Yes, potatoes, little Sunshine," I said, looking across the table at Steve, my brow creased with worry.

Dad took a sip of his coffee. I watched the brown liquid dribble out of the limp, drooping right side of his mouth and flow like a dirty rivulet in a deep groove down the side of his chin. He saw me looking at him and self-consciously wiped his chin with a napkin.

•••

Despite Dad's failing health, he and my mother continued to seek out that magical formula of adventure and service that had defined their early lives together. Later that same year, the failing hospital in Goessel, Kansas, where my dad had worked closed its doors. The folks decided to fly back to east Paraguay to restart their small rural practice there. But there were even fewer patients than before.

They then learned that the leprosy station at Km. 81 needed a doctor to fill in for a year. Joyful to be back in the work they had pioneered, they moved back into our L-shaped red brick house. But again, the experience was a painful one.

My mother wrote in a letter about their time at Km. 81, *The attitude of the personnel is negative toward Daddy. It seems they're not used to his demanding style. This is very hard for him.*

Their restlessness during those years reminded me of an Eagles song of that time, "Take It to the Limit." The lyrics of that song perfectly reflected the intensity with which my folks dreamed and stretched themselves beyond their limits, one more time, over and over again.

•••

I had been working toward an undergraduate degree in French and found that I was irresistibly drawn to the French language and culture. In ways that I didn't yet fully comprehend, my connection to French made me feel alive. My teacher encouraged me to attend a month-long course at the Sorbonne in Paris as part of my training. He said he would arrange everything. *But how would we afford the plane ticket? And what about the children?*

In December of 1979, at age twenty-eight, I got my chance. Steve's folks sent us money to come see them in India. We all spent Christmas and New Year's together with them in northern India. A few days after New Year's, I left alone for France to spend a month studying at the Sorbonne. Steve stayed on with the children in India, returning to the States with them a few weeks before I did.

Paris worked its way under my skin and into my soul. Even the cockroaches and rats in the shabby rented room I called home for a month didn't curb my passionate embrace of the city and its magic. Outside of my classes at the Sorbonne, I immersed myself in French live theater, which I could afford because of deeply discounted student theater passes. The great playwrights of seventeenth century France, Molière, Corneille, and especially Racine, drew me into their tragic worlds.

I fell in love with Phèdre, Racine's protagonist in the dramatic tragedy of the same name. She is a passionate lover, aware of nothing except her own anguish and the means by which she can relieve it. In the process, she causes immense suffering in others. But we also see her as an innocent victim. Racine successfully evokes contradictory feelings of pity and revulsion toward Phèdre. In the face of her horrific acts, there are intimations of overpowering forces—fate, a tainted heredity, and the absence of grace—all of which seem to make her more a victim than a sinner. She personifies one of Racine's most distinctive contributions to literature, his conception of the ambivalence of love: *"Ne puis-je savoir si j'aime, ou si je haïs?"* ("Can I not know whether I love or whether I hate?")

I wept through three different live performances of Phèdre during that month in Paris. And I stayed up late night after night reading the play numerous times from cover to cover. Phèdre stirred something deep within me. I longed to know what it would feel like to experience a love so intense it might be confused with hate. I yearned to feel something that fervently. To live that intensely. To open myself to a flood of passion that would nourish the dried-up and withered cells of my soul and penetrate the veil of numbness that had surrounded me for so long.

My entire being began to vibrate with a newfound vitality. But as the month in Paris drew to a close, that vibration began to feel more like raw fear. *Who had I become? And what would I do with who I had become once I was once again at home with my husband and children?*

Where I belonged.

•••

Steve and the children had driven to St. Louis to meet my flight from Europe. I squirmed in my seat as the plane began to descend. *What would it be like to see my family after this month of awakening? How would the children react to me? Had I been wrong to spend an entire month away from them?*

Shareen, then seven, ran toward me with open arms as I came through the jetway door. I threw my arms around her and drew her close to me.

Steve stood a ways back, holding three-year-old Stefan in his arms. I pulled my breath in sharply when I saw my baby boy. His entire face was raw, covered with pussy oozing sores and a few scabby areas.

"What happened?" I put my arms around both of them, searching Steve's eyes. "What happened to our baby?"

"He picked up something in India, Marlena. I've been to the doctor. There's nothing we can do but wait for the skin to heal," he said.

I rocked Stefan in my arms all the way back to our home in Champaign. "I'm so sorry, my sweet baby. I'm so sorry," I kept whispering into his ear. And inside of my head, so loud it was impossible for me to ignore, a stern voice scolded, "While you were off in Paris daydreaming about passions and love and hate, your little baby was suffering. What kind of a mother are you?"

Holding that dear child to my chest, I silently renewed my commitment to be a good wife and mother.

•••

I have a photo taken in the spring of 1980. I am standing with our two children in the front yard of our suburban home in Champaign, Illinois. We are dressed up to go to an Easter Sunday church service. I am clutching their hands, eight-year-old Shareen on my left and four-year-old Stefan on my right. My face is pretty enough, but blank, as if the woman in the photo has drawn blinds down over her face to keep everyone out, even the camera.

But the blinds were beginning to crack open.

CHAPTER 12:
It's Over (1980–1981)

Easter 1980

———

"I had finally made my choice, and so had he.
He let me go. I was relieved, which I expected.
What I didn't expect was to feel so much grief."

—Jenny Han, *We'll Always Have Summer*

———

It was a late afternoon in mid-August of 1980. Steve and the children and I were going to take the train to Newton, Kansas, to spend some time there with friends and relatives. The four of us sat around a Formica table at a booth in one corner of the café in the Galesburg, Illinois, train station. A faint stench of rancid grease hung in the air. Barry Manilow's otherwise velvety voice whined from a tinny speaker above our heads... *Oh Mandy...* Part of a rusty spring hung out of a gash in the brown vinyl seat cover next to me.

Without looking up from her tray, the waitress placed four tall plastic cups of water on the table in front of us.

"Can you please bring him a smaller cup?" I asked, nodding at four-year old Stefan. Only his blond mop of hair and greenish-blue eyes peered over the top of the table. Shareen, four years older and always his little mother, was trying to convince him to sit in a booster.

"It's OK, Shareen, he'll reach his food," Steve said, gently laying a hand on our daughter's arm.

Steve and I placed our orders and asked for hamburgers and fries from the kid's menu for the children.

"Look, Stefan," Shareen said. "See how you can make airplanes with these napkins?" The two of them, heads bent over a pile of paper napkins she had ripped out of the rusty metal napkin container, entered their own make-believe world.

I glanced at my husband sitting next to me, slightly slouched, hands in his lap. The dark gray sweater, the one I had given him for Christmas four years ago—or was it six?—bagged at his elbows.

In the booth next to us sat a couple carrying on an animated conversation. I watched the young woman leaning in toward her partner, laughing brightly. "I could hardly wait to tell you about..." I turned away, swallowing against a lump that stayed stuck in my throat.

The waitress brought our food. Shareen broke Stefan's burger into little pieces. Steve cut into his steak to check for doneness. The silence between us felt like the air in a coffin, and I wondered when it was that we'd run out of things to talk about. I stared into my bowl of chili, pushing the clumps of beans around with my spoon.

My mind began to wander. Everyone said ours was a good marriage. I agreed. But was good really enough? Was it asking too much to want a life partnership that provided more than safety? Was it too much to want a partner, as the poet Roy Croft said, who had the courage to put his hand deep into my heaped-up heart and, taking in all of the pathetic things that he couldn't help but see there, to draw out into the light all of the beautiful and radiant things that no one else ever looked quite deeply enough to find?

I again looked over at my husband, contentedly chewing on his steak in the booth next to me, and our children, who, having lost interest in their hamburgers, were back to making paper airplanes. *They are my world, these three*, I thought. *The family I dreamed of as a child when my parents were busy doing the Lord's work.*

Steve noticed me looking at him and slowly raised one brow. His kind brown eyes seemed to ask, "Is there something wrong?"

Nothing Bad Between Us

A shudder crawled down my spine, and I shook off the unthinkable, terrifying notion that in the midst of all of this serenity, something was painfully wrong.

I shook my head. "How's your steak, honey?" I asked, taking a small bite of my chili, which had grown cold.

•••

A few months later, Steve and I were sitting outside on our deck, sipping on beers and smoking cigarettes. The children were playing in the backyard with two wild Siamese cats they had adopted from the street. It was late fall, my favorite season. The rich, moist smell of dying leaves hung thick in the air, but it did little to lighten my heavy blanket of sadness.

"Please, Steve, I'm so unhappy. Can we find some help?" I pleaded.

Steve's warm chocolate-brown eyes turned to me, filled with deep sadness. "I just don't understand what we need help with. We have such a happy family," he said.

I tore my gaze away from those dear sad eyes. *How do I convey the deep well of emptiness inside of me when what he's happy about is that we get along and we don't fight? That can't be all that "happiness" means*, I thought to myself. Out loud I said, "I know..." My voice faltered. "Everybody says that. But I'm not happy, Steve. I feel hollow and empty."

Steve pulled long and hard on his cigarette. "I don't know how to help you, Marlena. I don't even know what you're asking of me."

I was silent, not knowing what more to say.

"Maybe we should find a church, get back to our Christian roots, pray together, that sort of thing. Maybe that would help," he said.

It was true that we had fallen completely away from our Christian roots. Prayer had never been a part of our family life, other than little rote prayers we said with our children at bedtime: *Now I lay me down to sleep. I pray thee, Lord, my soul to keep.*

I thought back to the Mennonite church of my youth and shuddered. "I can't imagine how going to church is going to help us, but if you think it might, I'm willing to try it."

We half-heartedly began attending a Methodist church, but prayer and devotion never really made their way into our lives. The dull hum of our daily routines continued. We supported each other in many practical ways. He cooked dinner or took the children to a park if I had to prepare for an exam. I spent summers alone with the kids when he sang in summer theaters around the country.

And through it all, I continued to shut down, a little bit at a time. I felt like I was married to a loving sibling, someone who cared for me, someone who kept me safe, like a brother might. No matter how safe it felt, for me our house in the suburbs had become a stage on which two adults and two children were playing out the make-believe game of a happy American family.

I ached for intimate connection, for the emotional intensity that had awakened within me briefly during my time in Paris.

•••

I had finished my undergraduate degree and was taking classes toward a PhD in French at the University of Illinois, often riding to the campus with Sue, my friend and neighbor across the street.

"Sue, everyone loves Steve. Why am I so unhappy?" I asked, caught up in a tangle of guilt and confusion.

"Everyone's not married to Steve," she said. She turned toward me and her brightly painted lips broke into a wide grin. I knew she was trying to lighten my self-absorbed dark mood.

"I just feel so stuck, Sue," I moaned. "I need to get out of this marriage. But how do you divorce the nicest man you've ever met?"

She shook her head. "I can't help you with that one," she said.

•••

Not long after that, I chose a coward's way out. "I've had an affair," I announced late one night, knowing that this would mark the end. The affair had been a senseless one-night stand. It had meant nothing to me. I must have known at some level that it would have enormous consequences. I did it anyway, knowing no other way to break free.

But the end felt devastating, not freeing.

For about a month after my announcement, we went through the motions of parenting together and carried on our lives as though in a trance. It took that long for Steve to find and rent an apartment. By then, his decision to end the marriage was resolute. He made an appointment with an attorney on the U of I campus who managed the divorce process for both of us. We both agreed that it made the most sense for me to have legal custody of the children, given how much time Steve spent in music theaters around the country. We didn't fight about any of the logistics of separation.

For me, the shocking finality of the rupture of my family felt almost too shattering to bear. One night, after the children were asleep, Steve and I sat side-by-side in two antique rocking chairs in our living room. A silent blanket of sadness enveloped both of us.

Tears spilled down over my cheeks. "Please, Steve. Would you reconsider? I'm so sorry about the affair, about what I've done to hurt you. I just can't bear the thought of losing this family," I said.

"I'm sorry. It's over," he said quietly.

I bent over in my rocker, feeling the room spin around me. *What had I done? What would I do now? And most terrifying of all, how would I tell my parents, for whom my marriage to Steve meant that I was finally acceptable to them?*

"Someday we'll all get together, your new family and my new family, and it will all be OK," Steve said gently.

I won't have any new family, I thought to myself. My tubes had been tied, and in any case, my little quarter of one ovary had already worked overtime. I would have no more children.

•••

It was toward the end of April or maybe early May of 1981. Steve had not yet found an apartment and was still living with us, though we slept in separate bedrooms. Illinois spring showers had left a rich musty smell of wet soil. As though ignoring the impending divorce, my husband and I moved forward with putting in a flower garden we had planned for the front yard. A peony bush was already yielding large deep rose-colored balls. New river rock finished the areas between the flowerbeds. Steve was a natural at gardening, and I was a strong laborer by his side. We also planted those smelly little marigolds, though I wasn't sure why. Were they to keep the rabbits away? Slugs?

Sweating in that garden next to my husband filled me with unfounded hope that things could still work out. We worked well together. The beauty we created so naturally side-by-side reminded me of all that was still true and good about our marriage.

That night in late April or early May, Steve got drunk across the street with the husband of my friend Sue. Sue informed me the next morning that Steve had told her husband all about his new love Becky. He had already found someone else and was moving on.

•••

It was time to tell the children about our divorce. I had just finished baking chocolate chip cookies. The fresh-baked aroma still hung in the air. The four of us sat around our round pressed-wood oak table in the kitchen. Stefan was busy washing down his cookie with a glass of milk. I looked over at Steve, not knowing who should start, nor exactly what we should say. We hadn't discussed how we were going to do this. He avoided my eyes.

"Mommy and I...uh... Mommy and I, we're getting a divorce," he said. His shoulders were hunched over. His soft brown eyes seemed clouded as they fell on his two children.

Shareen's eyes grew very large and she looked from one of us to the other and then back again. Back and forth her eyes darted, her mouth partly open, silent. Hanging from the side arms of her eyeglass frames were rows and rows of little beaded safety pins, the latest fashion among her eight-year-old friends.

Stefan put down his glass of milk. "Can I please have 'nother cookie, Mommy?" he asked, not understanding what had just come down.

That's when it exploded out of Shareen's mouth, "Please don't tell Rita and Bill. I don't ever want Christine to know." She sat at the edge of her chair, hands clutched in her lap, cookie ignored.

I reached out to hug the child that Steve and my quarter of an ovary had miraculously conceived almost ten years ago in Paraguay. She stiffened. Steve's eyes seemed focused on something in his lap.

Although I wasn't yet fully aware of it at the time, my daughter's plea to not tell her best friend's parents accurately reflected the farce of the home in which we had been raising her. We had successfully spun a story of the perfect family. Every one of our friends and family members was shocked when we announced our divorce. Our deceptive games had gone far beyond hiding booze and cigarettes from our folks. They had spread to what Steve and I wanted each other and everyone else to believe: We have a happy marriage.

•••

A few weeks later, Steve took the children to see his parents in Florida to give them the news of our divorce in person. I didn't question his decision to go. I no longer felt I had the right or the privilege to question anything he did. As though in a trance, I prepared food for their trip: ham sandwiches, with lots of mustard the way he liked them, fried chicken, which was Shareen's favorite, and lots of cut-up fruit.

I stood on our front stoop and watched the brown Pinto back out of our driveway. Steve looked straight ahead. The children both waved goodbyes. I dropped to the ground and just sat there for a long time among the brightly colored rose and peonies bushes my soon-to-be-ex-husband and I had planted.

•••

With Steve and the children gone, I was left to deal with the most frightening part of the divorce: writing the letter to my parents.

Dear Mom and Dad, I began. *I have some sad news...* Saliva pooled in my mouth, and I ran to the bathroom and retched.

I tore up the letter and began another one. *My heart is heavy*, I wrote. This one, too, I threw away. After four tries, I put aside the pen and paper. Huge sobs exploded from my chest. I curled up on my living room floor.

I was unaware of time passing. At one point, in a thick fog, I heard that someone had opened the front door and was coming up the short flight of steps of our bi-level house.

My friend Sue gasped as she stared down at me, coiled into a fetal position on the floor. "I have been trying to call you all day. What are you doing?" She screamed at me.

I didn't respond.

"Marlena, what are you doing?" She yelled louder. It worked. I slowly lifted my head, but it felt like an enormous rock, separated from my body, and it dropped back onto the floor.

"You look awful. Are you sick? I'm sorry I yelled at you. I was just so worried. Should I take you to the hospital?" Her voice softened and she laid one hand on my shoulder.

"Uh-uh," I moaned. And then I remembered where I was and why there was no point in living anymore. "Steve has taken the kids to Florida to see his parents and tell them we're divorcing. I begged him to reconsider, that there must still be some hope, that…" My voice cracked and I mumbled into the carpet, "There's no reason for me to go on living."

Sue, my ever-so-practical friend, went to the kitchen to pour me a glass of water. "When's the last time you ate or drank anything?"

I couldn't remember. My head was pounding, and the massive weight bearing down on my chest constricted my breathing.

Her dark eyes flared. "How dare you do this? You say your kids are more important to you than anything else? Then how can you say there's no reason to go on?"

She pulled me up off the floor, pushed me into a chair, and handed me a glass of water. "Here, drink this and quit being so damned self-centered. You say you're a good mom. *Be* a good mom and take care of yourself so you're here when they get back."

•••

Finally, I wrote the letter.

We have tried to get help, I wrote, faltered and then decided to just go for it. *Steve and I are getting a divorce.*

The last paragraph of that letter (which my mother gave me before she died in 2010—she kept it all those years?) read,

> *I thank God for our children. They are the only thing left in my life that has any meaning for me now. When each morning I lie paralyzed in my bed, thinking I can't face another day, I think of them, of my love for them, and my responsibility to them, and somehow, I find the strength. I am truly and deeply sorry for the pain I know this will cause you too.*

CHAPTER 13:

Spinning out of Control (1981–1986)

Hitting rock bottom

———

"Maybe all one can do is hope to end up with the right regrets."

—Arthur Miller

———

It took weeks for airmail letters to reach my folks in Paraguay. So it was more than a month before I heard back from them. My fingers shook as I ripped open the thin blue airmail envelope, almost destroying the letter in the process. *Would they once again disown me? Was it even possible for them to love me without their beloved Steve?*

The first part of the letter was in my father's bold handwriting.

> *We are very concerned about the decision you have made. It is not God's will that a man and wife break their vows. We are truly disappointed in you. You have sinned, and that will not go unpunished. But at least you did not write to say that you are a lesbian.*

The letter continued in this vein, my mother adding her list of ways that

I was once again a disappointment to them. At age thirty, I had come full circle in the decade since I left Paraguay. I remembered my mother's words as she had tearfully hugged me goodbye in 1970 at the *Puerto Presidente Stroessner* airport in Asunción. "You are a sick child. I pray that you will find your way." In their eyes, I was that sick child again.

I had fallen a long way from the rule-bound self-righteous young girl I had been in Asunción. I had lived within the bounds of strict rules in my Mennonite family. And even when I had no one imposing those rules on me while living on my own in Asunción, I initially flaunted my adherence to the good Mennonite rulebook and held myself as well as those around me accountable. But when I broke the most sacred of all rules, when I had that affair with Hans, all of the rules lost their hold over me. Once there was a crack in the Mennonite gestalt that was my life, I became rudderless.

•••

During my ten-year marriage to Steve, we had both focused on getting him through graduate school and launched into a career as an opera singer, director, and music professor. I had an undergraduate degree in French. I still loved everything French. My dream had been to get a PhD in French Literature.

But now I was the primary provider for my two children. The small amount of child support Steve could afford to give me didn't begin to make ends meet. Pragmatism as well as raw fear pushed me out of the French Department at the University of Illinois and across the central quadrangle, to what I thought of as the dark side. But an MBA would give me more earning power. I entered Commerce "Com" West, the building that housed the university's College of Commerce and Business Administration. The French Department had been a comfortable, laid-back, mostly women's world. When I walked through the dark and imposing doors of Com West, I entered what was a foreign realm for me and at the time a still predominantly male world of MBAs.

My first class in Com West was calculus. I took a seat in the back of the room, hoping no one would notice that I didn't belong there with my long

Nothing Bad Between Us

kinky red hair and my overly casual jeans and sweatshirt. The professor, a short wiry young man with dark-rimmed glasses, briskly walked in and dropped his books on the table in front of the room. He barely glanced at us. This felt nothing at all like the warm and welcoming "*Bon jour. Ça va?*" at the other end of the campus.

I am assuming that all of you have had at least two semesters of algebra." Without waiting for an answer, he continued, "Consider a function $y = f(x)$ and its graph. As you know, the graph of a function is a set of points." He turned to the chalkboard and wrote $(x, f(x))$. "I can draw the graph in a plane with a horizontal axis, which you know is the x-axis. And a vertical axis, which you know is..."

My vision blurred until I could no longer clearly see the axes he was charting on the board and his words faded away. I felt my chest pounding. Why had I ever thought I could do this? I had never taken any algebra, and no, I didn't know that the graph of a function was a set of... Hell, I didn't even know what this thing called a "function" was.

I shook my head as if to dislodge cobwebs from my brain and looked around me. Rows of men, most of them seeming to be much younger than I, sat nonchalantly at their desks, looking almost bored. One guy in particular, a bit disheveled compared to the rest of the MBA crowd, slouched in his chair, his eyes half closed as though he was taking a nap.

I heard nothing else the professor said during that first class. But when class ended ninety minutes later, I had a plan.

"Hi, my name is Marlena," I said to the napper as we were leaving the classroom.

"I'm Tim," he said and started to move past me.

"Hey, please wait. I have a question." My voice came out higher-pitched than I wanted it to, almost a wail. "You look like you know the stuff the professor was talking about. My algebra is just a little rusty. Can you tell me which algebra books I might look at to brush up a bit?"

Tim's hair was all mussed up like he never combed it. His pants were baggy. He didn't look as slick as the rest of the MBA crowd. He looked quizzically at me, as though trying to decide whether or not I was serious.

I bought the two books Tim recommended and I studied them on my own, late into each night, until I had fully consumed both of them. Occasionally I would ask him for help with a particularly difficult set of formulas.

"I hate this stuff," I complained one afternoon, as Tim and I sat across from each other at my dining room table. Stefan, who had just turned six, was sitting on the floor near us, mouthing the words he was learning to read from the latest comic book Tim had brought him. Shareen was outside playing with her best friend Christine. "I can't believe I'm doing this."

Tim grinned that lopsided smile of his, "You never took any algebra before, did you, Red? You've come a long way, baby."

• • •

The years at Com West are mostly a blur for me now. I taught undergraduate courses in Business Writing for the English Department and Management courses for the College of Business and Administration in order to waive my tuition fees and earn a few dollars. After attending my classes, I hurried home in time to be there when the children arrived from school. One day a week, I was a teacher's aide at their grade school. I helped with homework, refereed the many sibling fights, wiped snotty noses, kissed away tears, and told bedtime stories. Late into each night, coffee and cigarettes provided the fuel that kept me awake to tackle my schoolwork.

On schedule, I had my MBA degree in hand. But the thought of being a marketing or operations manager at Kraft Foods or Caterpillar International, two of the companies that actively recruited Illinois MBAs, held no appeal. In fact, it repulsed me. So I continued on. My earlier dream had been to earn a PhD in French Literary Criticism. I could still be an academic, I now decided, but in business, which eventually would better allow me to pay the bills.

For a while, I was able to devote every other weekend completely to my studies when the children were with Steve and his new wife Becky. But then one day that changed.

Steve called. "Shareen and Stefan are constantly bickering and I don't know how to get them to stop it. Becky and I really can't tolerate their fighting. From now on, we want to have only one of them come to our house at a time," he said as matter-of-factly as though he were talking about the weather.

"What do you mean 'you want to have only one of them at a time'?" I asked, not believing I had heard correctly.

"Just what I said. One weekend, Shareen can come alone. Two weeks later, Stefan can come."

"But Steve, I need those free weekends to catch up on my studies. It's not..." I started.

He interrupted me, "You're the one who wanted custody."

•••

During those years, I honed the game of deception that Steve and I had learned to play so well. My parents and I didn't see one another very often, so I could easily keep from them the nasty little truths about my life that would prove my true depravity: I smoked. I drank. I screwed around. Hungry for intimate connection, one night I even tried to stoop to the lowest rung of my father's ladder of sins.

With my friend Annelle.

Annelle and I had met the previous year. We had both studied Semiotics in the French PhD program at the University of Illinois and still kept in touch. We each saw much of ourselves reflected in the other: poor, divorced, single mom; horny and lonely.

One day, she stopped me as we passed each on the university quadrangle. "Marlena, I've been thinking a lot about what you told me. You know...about feeling so dead in your marriage and then still feeling just as dead now that it's over." She paused, glancing nervously around us. Quickly she continued, "Would you like to come over to my place sometime when we don't have our kids with us? Would you like to...you know..." She leaned in closer to me, her dark brown eyes drilling into mine, as though begging me to understand what she meant so she wouldn't have to say it out loud.

We came up with a plan, and there I was, in her three-room apartment just a few blocks from campus. The front room was sparsely furnished. We sat on oversized pillows on the floor. A dozen or so candles flickered, casting eerie shadows in the dusky twilight. A long low coffee table stood in the middle of the room, covered with stacks of books and papers. I put down my glass and flipped through a few of the familiar titles. Umberto Eco's *The Name of the Rose*. Michel Foucault's *Les Mots et les Choses*. I wished Annelle weren't sitting quite so close to me. I wondered if she could see my fingers shaking as I nonchalantly turned the pages, wondered if she saw my lips tremble as I silently read from the first page of Foucault's *Préface*, "*Qu'est-il donc impossible de penser...*"

We clinked our wine glasses. "To us," we said in unison, with a bravado I wasn't feeling. My eyes dropped from Annelle's face to take in the way her starched white button-down shirt accented her deeply tanned neck and chest. She had left the top two buttons undone, exposing the cleavage of her breasts, which proudly jutted out despite having nursed a baby many years ago. I felt self-conscious about my own breasts that were soft and limp after nursing my two.

"Marlena, stop." Annelle took the book from my hands. As she moved her body sideways to place it on the table, I could make out her nipples, dark and hard against the light cotton fabric of her shirt. She looked sexy as hell.

I gripped my glass of wine in both hands and downed what was left in it.

Annelle rose from the cushion. "I'll get the bottle," she said, making her way to the kitchen.

She returned with the wine bottle, refilled both of our glasses and sat down next to me on my pillow, her upper left thigh resting against my leg. I felt a hot ripple surge through my body. Annelle's hand reached tentatively toward the zipper of my jeans. I sucked in my breath.

She paused, her hand not yet on me. I reached across her for my wine glass, drank too quickly, and choked. I coughed loudly and spewed red wine all over her pillows and floor.

"I...I'm so sorry." I continued to cough and sputter.

Annelle burst out laughing. Within seconds, we were both rolling on the floor, laughing until we cried. "I wish it could have worked. I wanted it to so much." Annelle gasped through fits of laughter.

"Me too." I pulled myself up off the floor, trying to stifle the giggling that still bordered on hysteria.

"Maybe we're stuck with men after all," I said after we regained our composure and started on our third glass of wine.

Annelle's eyes darkened. She blurted, "I still hate men."

"I'll drink to that," I said, and this time, we clinked our wine glasses with much greater certainty.

•••

Three months later, I met Joe at his former girlfriend's party.

The lights were turned down so low that I could barely distinguish one from another among the undulating bodies dancing to "I Still Haven't Found What I'm Looking For." The living room reeked of smoke and beer. I opened the squeaky screen door leading out to the front porch.

"Do you wanna blow this joint, cowboy?" Joe sat on the porch swing, staring at me as I came through the door. His muscled lean arms were draped over the back of the swing. Tight jeans accentuated a narrow waist and long legs.

I knew his name. He had been in one of my MBA classes. I also knew he was a popular student, especially among the girls. He and I had danced to AC/DC's "You Shook Me All Night Long" earlier that evening. One dance.

He moved over and I sat down beside him. "Where do you want to go?" I asked, not sure that I understood. I was a thirty-two-year-old woman. He was much younger than I, a party boy, someone certainly not interested in someone like me. And what would he think if he learned I had kids?

"Your place or mine?" His deep brown bedroom eyes drilled into mine.

That night in his apartment, my body devoured his fluids like parched earth soaking up the rain. I was unquenchable and he kept on delivering.

Early the next morning I jerked awake, remembering that the kids would be home by ten o'clock.

"Gotta go," I mumbled, awkwardly pulling on my clothes. I felt so sore after our time together I could hardly walk.

"When will I see you again?" Joe asked, lazily pushing his tanned naked limbs out from under the sheet.

I didn't know what to say. I didn't want this to be a one-night stand. But how could it possibly be anything else? I was too old for this boy, and I had a seven-year-old son and an eleven-year-old daughter he didn't even know about.

"Not sure, Joe. Why don't I call you?" I headed unsteadily for the door.

Over the course of the next few months, Joe and I met whenever I could find care for the children. Steve was a good father, but he didn't often have time to be with them, especially not with the two of them together. But whenever we got a chance, Joe and I created our own little bubble, separate from my real life.

He didn't seem to mind that I was a mother of two, and whenever he was around the children, which wasn't often, they got along well. We didn't talk much about the kids. In fact, we didn't talk much about any part of my real life of being a single parent, of buying our clothes at the Goodwill store or of eating nothing but peanut butter and jelly sandwiches at the end of the month before my teaching-assistant paycheck came in.

"I'm losing my apartment," Joe said one night, as we lay exhausted next to each other. "What if I move in with you? I could help you cover some of your mortgage payment."

"I don't know...my children..." I started.

"Your kids have a good dad," he interrupted. "I won't disrupt their lives. I'm not worried about that."

The next day I brought the subject up with Shareen. Stefan was still a young child. But at eleven, Shareen was already showing signs of becoming a woman. How would she feel about me bringing a man home to live with us?

"But will he be like our dad?" she asked, a worried crease across her forehead.

"No. No one will ever be like your dad except your dad," I said with certainty.

She was satisfied with that, and Stefan liked Joe a lot. So he moved in. It was just as Joe had promised. He didn't disrupt my children's lives. He was not "like their dad." He and I cooked together, studied together, and helped each other financially. He left the parenting to me. When I spent time with the kids, helping them with homework, reading to them, or taking them to their various lessons, Joe hung out with his friends or did his homework. And every night we entered our own little private bubble and it nourished me.

Joe finished his MBA a year before I finished my PhD coursework. A company in Connecticut offered him a job.

"Marry me," he said, falling to his knees. We were in the sunken gardens at Allerton Park, a 1,500-acre nature center and conference retreat center owned by the University of Illinois. "Before I take the job in Connecticut, I want to know that we'll be together after you finish your course work next year."

I wanted him. I would miss him terribly. We had figured out a way to be together that seemed to work for everyone. For him, for me, for the kids. And at thirty-two, as a mother of two, I wondered if I would get many more chances at romance.

"Yes, I will marry you," I said, allowing him to wrap his arms around my waist and pull me close to him.

We lived a fairy tale that year. Joe's salary allowed us to fly to see one another at least once a month, whenever I could convince Steve to take both of the children or got a babysitter to stay with them. We were completely carefree during those weekends. We ate in restaurants I had never been able to afford. We saw shows I had never dreamed of seeing. It was as though I was capturing some of the lighthearted life I had never had in the Mennonite world of my youth. During those weekends, we created the ultimate dream world far from the demanding realities of my work, studies, and child rearing.

•••

The wedding was a week away. Joe had taken time off from work and had been back in Champaign at my house for the past week. We were busy planning the ceremony and wedding party, packing up the house, and arranging to move everything to Connecticut right after the event.

"Why haven't your kids packed the stuff in their rooms yet?" Joe asked, stomping out of Shareen's room and slamming the door behind him.

"Shareen's been busy with school, and..." My voice trailed off. Joe had already walked out of the house. I sank heavily into the nearest chair. *What was happening?* I thought back to the months Joe had lived with us prior to leaving for Connecticut. It had been so easy. He hardly seemed to notice the kids, and that was fine with me. He had been in love with me and had doted on me, with roses and chocolates, the works. Our romance had only intensified when we were apart for most of the entire past year. But that romance had been childless.

Now that all of us were together in the same house again and Joe and I were about to be married, everything seemed wrong. The children had been edgy all week, not used to having Joe around. He was constantly critical of them. And I had become anxious and irritable.

One by one, friends and family members began to arrive in town for the wedding, and with each arrival, my anxiety grew. Each one further closed off the possibility of turning back and declaring it all a mistake.

Especially when my folks showed up.

They had again moved from Paraguay back to Goessel, Kansas, earlier that year. I knew that Dad's health problems continued. He looked more worn down than I had ever seen him. Just the previous month, he had returned to the Mayo Clinic for prostate surgery. The morning he was to check out, he felt miserable; he was nauseated and vomiting. My mother said he had talked to her about what kind of coffin he wanted.

It also seemed to me that for the first time in their lives, my folks were turning to their family for meaning in their lives. In a recent letter to me, Dad wrote, *Having Mary Lou* [my younger sister who lived in Kansas] *and her family close brings to mind the need for developing relationships.* And farther down on the page, he added, *We don't feel worthy of our children and grandchildren...often we have failed you.*

I thought about that letter. Reading those words, my knees had felt like they would crumple underneath me, and my chest had constricted. *Was this Dad's way of saying he was sorry for beating me so hard? Sorry about so often not being there for me?*

During the phone call earlier in the year when I had announced my plan to marry Joe, Dad was mostly silent. Mom asked over and over again in different ways, "Have you prayed about this and do you really feel that this is the Lord's will?" Toward the end of the call, after a moment of awkward silence, Dad cleared his throat and said, "We will be there and we will offer you our blessing."

And here they were. But now I had seriously begun to doubt the wisdom of my decision. I wished I could talk with them about it, but I didn't know how.

The wedding was a gala affair. My folks were gracious and loving, even when the champagne flowed, and the dancing began. They sat off to the side with my sister Mary Lou and her family, not taking part in the sinful behaviors of drinking and dancing, but also not seeming the least bit judgmental.

That warm summer night, as my brand-new husband lay snoring in his half-drunken sleep, I sat on the windowsill of a wide-open window in our motel room and sobbed.

•••

"Get your butt in here and clean up this mess!" Joe yelled at Shareen, who crouched back into a corner of the kitchen. "How many times do I have to tell you to clean up after yourself?"

Joe and I had been married for two years. We had moved from Connecticut to New Jersey, making it easier for us to commute to our jobs in Manhattan. Joe now worked for Chase Manhattan Bank, and I had just landed a position on the business school faculty at New York University (NYU).

This had become an all too familiar scene. "Joe, please, let me talk to her," I pleaded.

"You don't control your daughter, so I have to," he said. "Now get over here and get moving." Roughly, he pushed Shareen over to the counter.

I swallowed hard and left the room, the familiar guilt and anger pressing against my chest.

That night when we were alone, I confronted him as I had many times before. "You said you would leave the parenting of my children to their father and me," I began. "I just can't tolerate the way..."

The bedroom door slammed behind him as Joe left the room and locked himself into the bathroom. Twenty minutes later he climbed into bed and turned his back to me.

"Joe, please...can we...?"

"I don't want or need you now. I just want to go to sleep," he said, pulling his pillow over his head.

When he was asleep, I got out of bed and went into the bathroom, knowing I would find the sticky wadded-up tissues he always left behind. I flushed them down the toilet so the kids wouldn't see them in the morning. I thought about the many times over the past two years Joe and I had been to therapists and had discussed how hurtful this behavior was to me. How many times Joe had promised it would never happen again. And how disgusting the left-behind evidence of the betrayal of those promises always was.

Our constant fights about my children did nothing to protect them from him. The fights only made him lash out more harshly toward them, especially Shareen.

And to withhold sex from me: that was his weapon.

•••

It was a warm spring evening. We had eaten an early dinner. The children were upstairs working on homework. Joe and I were sipping a glass of wine in the back yard. Our two dogwood trees were heavy with pink blossoms. Their scent hung thick in the air. I took a deep breath. It had been a long time since it had felt this peaceful in our home.

Shareen stepped off the back porch and called out to us, "I'm going next door for a bit."

"Not until you sweep the kitchen floor," Joe yelled back.

By then she was out the door. Joe jumped out of his chair and ran after her. I was right behind him. As he crossed through the kitchen, I grabbed his arm and pulled him back. He wrenched himself free of my grip, lifted a metal spatula from the counter and hurled it at me. It flew past my face and cut a deep gouge into the wall behind me.

We stood there in the middle of the kitchen, silently glaring at each other, both of us stunned by what had just taken place.

That night, as I lay seething on my side of the bed, Joe didn't leave the bedroom to lock himself into the bathroom. Instead, he sat up and turned toward me. "You want sex? Is that what you want? Here!"

I was lying on my back. He roughly pushed me over onto my belly. As I cried out in pain, I vowed to myself to find a way out.

Nothing Bad Between Us

•••

The children were with Steve for the summer when Joe moved out. I was both grateful they weren't there and terribly sad to be without them at this time.

I felt none of the brokenness I had experienced when Steve and I split up. Instead, I felt furious rage, a fire that was stuffed so deep into my chest and burned so intensely that at times it was suffocating.

I was angry all the time. At everything. At the weather. At the mailman for being late. At the grocery store attendant for smiling too much. During that entire summer, fury consumed my days and my nights.

On a dark stormy evening in early August, about three months after Joe left, the smoldering rage finally exploded. I was alone in the house. Lightning streaked across the sky, followed by a loud crack of thunder. I thought I was headed for the kitchen to prepare myself a salad. Instead, I flung open the back door and ran out into our backyard, the rain pelting down on me. I threw myself onto the muddy ground, fists pounding madly into the muck.

"I hate you, Joe!" I screamed and screamed. "*I hate, hate, hate you, Dad! I hate you God...*" This went on and on, my fingers clawing frantically at the mud. I don't know how long I lay there. Thankfully the storm kept my piercing shouts from reverberating throughout the neighborhood.

A particularly loud clap of thunder finally penetrated my rage. *What am I saying? What am I doing out here in the storm? And how dare I rant against my father, the man who had saved my left ovary and then ushered my miraculous first child into this world?*

The pent-up raging fire in my chest had dissipated for now. In its place was a cavernous well of sadness so deep it seemed bottomless. I sat up. Throwing my arms tightly around my broken body, my mud-caked hands grasping each shoulder, I stumbled back into the house, head bent down against the pounding rain.

That night, as the storm slowly subsided into a drizzle, I lay curled up alone in a fetal position in my big king-sized bed. For hours, I sobbed like a young child, wishing I could again be that little girl and have it turn out differently, wishing I could make it all better for Daddy and me.

In the morning, anger once again filled up the enormous hole deep inside of me, pushing aside the fleeting waves of sadness and tenderness.

•••

This time the letter to my parents was easier to write. They had seen me suffer for over two years. More importantly, they had seen my children suffer.

You did the right thing to get a divorce, my father wrote back. *You've made a lot of really bad mistakes in your life, but you have always been a good mother. You are right to protect your children. You have been through a lot. Mom and I are here to support you any way we can.*

I held that letter against my heart like it was my lifeline. "Thank you, Dad." I breathed in deeply. "Thank you for not giving up on me."

CHAPTER 14:
Picking Up the Pieces (1986–1988)

I did it—but not on my own

_____

"Everyone who is arrogant in heart
is an abomination to the Lord."

—Proverbs 16:5, The Bible

_____

"What's symbiotics?" My father asked, looking perplexed. I was explaining to my parents that I had based my management doctoral dissertation on a methodology I had learned while studying French literature and that I was now attempting to publish the study in the highest-ranked journal of the management field.

"Semiotics, Dad." I was excited that he was actually asking me something about my research. Most of the time, the folks simply smiled when I mentioned what I was working on, vague smiles, the kind that made me sure they weren't really interested. "It's a methodology I learned for analyzing French texts. Semioticians study words or other signs as part of semiotic sign systems to analyze how meanings are made. They are concerned..." I stopped when I saw the glazed look on his face. "Anyway, I'm pretty excited that I was able to apply something hardly anybody knows about in the business world," I concluded limply.

There was an awkward silence. The folks had come to visit the children and me in New Jersey. The three of us were sitting around my kitchen table, drinking the customary cup of coffee they always drank after their afternoon nap.

I coughed nervously. "Well, my major advisor told me I would have trouble selling myself based on something this unknown and unfamiliar. I know it's kinda weird."

"I'm sure you're doing a good job, honey," my mother said, patting my arm.

"Just be sure you don't get prideful about it," Dad said gruffly. "You know it says in the book of Isaiah that Satan was cast out of heaven because of pride. Pride is giving yourself the credit for something that God has accomplished. Pride is taking the glory that belongs to God alone and keeping it for yourself."

"I know, Dad," I said, my enthusiasm depleted.

I thought about how strongly I felt that I had accomplished something really important by getting through a PhD program and securing a great job in the highly ranked business school at NYU all on my own, all while supporting my two children. *All on my own.* Really? I heard my father's words ringing in my head: *Pride is giving yourself the credit for what God has accomplished.*

Dad's voice broke into my thoughts. "Marlena, we wanted to talk to you about something that has been on our minds." He glanced across the table at my mother and then continued. "Are you teaching your children good Christian principles?" His eyes were now bright with intensity. "You know, Shareen is a teenager by now and Stefan not far behind. There are many temptations out there. They need the Lord's guidance."

I wasn't sure about the "Lord's guidance" thing, but I had given a lot of thought to my children's spiritual development. I wanted them to understand the various religious traditions of the world. And I wanted them to make informed choices about which spiritual path made sense to them. But I knew that for my parents there was only one path to God.

I cleared my throat. "Yes, we go to church," I said, hoping they wouldn't ask *what* church.

Worse. "Can we all go together to your church this Sunday?"

Nothing Bad Between Us

Inwardly I groaned but managed a smile. Although taking them to my church was the last thing I wanted to do, I saw no way to get out of it. "Yes, of course."

•••

That Sunday, as we walked through the front doors of our Unitarian Universalist church, I saw it for the first time as I knew my parents were seeing it, through the eyes of a devout Mennonite. People were not sitting in their pews, silently prayerful, waiting for the service to begin. They were milling about, greeting each other, laughing and talking animatedly. There was no quiet organ music taking people into a still place of prayer. A pianist came through the side door and began playing a honky-tonk tune, at which point people sort of formed a circle around and between the chairs and everyone began to sing boisterously, "We Are Standing on the Side of Love." Some people clapped. Others danced to the catchy tune.

I glanced sideways at my parents standing next to me without turning my head toward them. They were staring at the scene before them, their mouths hanging partially open.

A young woman rose and faced the audience. "Greetings and welcome to our open and inclusive community of faith," she began.

"That's your pastor?" I heard my father whisper. I realized she didn't look pastoral at all in the Mennonite sense. She even wore worldly jewelry and makeup. This wasn't going well at all.

And then it got even worse. A guest speaker gave a talk (we Unitarian Universalists didn't refer to them as sermons) about a meeting with the Dalai Lama. He showed slides and told us how moved he had been by the Dalai Lama's message of peace.

"The Dalai Lama is so down-to-earth, relaxed, and even playful," he said.

I squirmed. *Why couldn't he have chosen to talk about a meeting with Jesus, or something, anything more Christian-like?*

The service ended with more lively music. I knew it had been a huge mistake to bring the folks.

"He didn't say one word about Jesus Christ or God in his entire talk," Dad said as we walked to the car. "I just don't see how that can be a Christian church."

Back at home, the kids and I were cleaning up the lunch dishes. My parents had gone upstairs to take a nap.

Stefan stopped drying a plate and looked at me. "*Grosspa* is so smart, and he says we won't go to heaven unless we believe in Jesus Christ as our Savior. Do you think he might be right, Mom?"

I sensed Shareen's eyes on me. "He *is* so smart, Stefan," I said. "But you know, smarts aren't really what lead the way when it comes to our spiritual beliefs. He's a Mennonite through and through, your grandfather, and there'll only ever be one truth for him."

Shareen seemed to ponder this, her hands still submerged in the soapy water in the sink, her head down. "I just wish we didn't have to be Christians for *Grossma* and *Grosspa* to think we're good people. I mean, we're just as nice as all the other cousins, but somehow..." She stopped, resuming the dishwashing with more oomph than before.

I wrapped my arms around my daughter, noticing how quickly she was developing into a shapely young woman. "Oh, my dear Shareen, I do understand what you're saying, and I am so, so sorry. You are a good person, no matter what your beliefs are about religion. Please believe me."

•••

Despite the uncomfortable conversations about Christianity, I began to look forward to the visits, both in my parents' house in Goessel and at our house in New Jersey. We played endless games of UNO. The folks told colorful stories about their lives in Paraguay that charmed my kids. Mom baked my favorite, banana cream pie. I made Dad's favorite, fried potatoes for breakfast. We seemed to have begun a tenuous new way of relating to one another.

One cool spring day, my younger sister Mary Lou, who lived near our parents in Kansas, picked us up at the Wichita airport and took us to their home in Goessel. The little house had been my grandmother's home decades earlier. The exterior was old and worn, with chipped yellow painted siding. Inside was just as tired. A tiny kitchen with a linoleum floor (with a few bare spots where the linoleum had broken away), a chipped Formica countertop, and a small round foldout wooden table. The rust-colored living room shag carpet was worn smooth in a line from the front door to the kitchen. Two small bedrooms and an even smaller bathroom (with a rusty bathtub and basin) made up the rest of the house.

Dilapidated. Tired. And yet somehow so warm and inviting.

My folks were standing on their broken-down front porch waiting for us when my sister pulled into their gravel driveway. Mom was wearing a faded cotton print dress and Dad had on a pair of brown, slightly bell-bottomed polyester pants that looked like they were from the 1970s and about three inches too short. He had probably bought them at a thrift shop.

We piled out of the car and the kids ran to them.

"*Grossma, Grosspa!*" Even though they were eleven and fifteen years old, a time in life when grandparents are often not terribly interesting, and despite the concerns about not being Christians and therefore less likeable, my two seemed to love being around my parents.

"How about a game of UNO?" And off they went. *How did my folks become so gentle, so loving, so interested in playing games, so into just having a good time?* I wondered. *Was I asleep to when things changed? How long had it been going on?* It was as if the attention they were unable to give me as a child now poured out onto my children. With every game they played and every story they told, fragments of our broken relationship seemed to pull back together.

I began to observe them more closely when we were all together. Dad would always do the dishes after supper, something I never remembered him doing when I was a kid. Even though their little kitchen was barely large enough to accommodate all three of them, Shareen and Stefan would rinse and dry while he washed. Mom would buzz in and out to put the dishes away.

"Did you two ever hear the story about how the Mennonites escaped from Russia in the late 1800s?" he asked them.

They had, many times, but good-humoredly said, "Tell us about that, *Grosspa*." So he launched enthusiastically into his favorite story about the persecutions, the drought, the illnesses, the strong faith, and finally the arrival of his grandparents Jacob and Lena, along with a large Mennonite clan, in Kansas in 1874, right here in this little town of Goessel.

"What does it really mean to be a Mennonite?" asked Shareen. I blushed and wanted to hide, wondering what my father must think of me. *My grandchildren don't know what it means to be Mennonite?*

But he seemed unperturbed and not in the least surprised.

"To be a Mennonite means above all to believe that Jesus Christ is your Savior," he said. "And it also means that we are pacifists."

"What's a pacifist?" Stefan asked.

"It means we don't kill. We don't believe in the use of force. We don't even join an army," he replied softly, patient with my children's ignorance about this most important issue.

I stood apart, listening and watching. A lump formed in my throat. "I'll be back," I said, grabbing my jacket that had a pack of Marlboros hidden in one of the pockets.

I walked to a small deserted Mennonite cemetery I knew about, less than a mile outside of town. As I made my way through the uneven rows of broken-down headstones, I pulled hard on my cigarette and read the epitaphs. *Why do I feel so unhinged?* I wondered. *So disoriented?* I had had my armor up for so long, warding off my father's attacks and wanting to maintain my illusion of control, it was confusing for me not to need it anymore. He and my mother both seemed tired, even frail. And tender.

I sat on the ground near a tiny headstone that read "Johann Wedel" and, under the name, the years 1901–1903. I lit another cigarette and closed my eyes. The jumbled events of my life seemed to take on different shapes, like the arbitrary patterns that show up in a kaleidoscope when several mirrors are placed at an angle to one another. I loved Dad so very much, and it seemed to me that I was always trying to please him. At the same time, I had disappointed him over and over again, and at least until now, had continuously tried to escape his judgments. But was that changing?

"Ah, Dad," I said aloud to the headstones and to the wheat fields beyond. "You were pretty full of contradictions yourself." He was always such a staunch pacifist, even going to Washington DC to meet with Kansas Senator Brownback about the Peace Tax Fund. And when Shareen had asked earlier, "What does it really mean to be a Mennonite?" his answer, of course, as always, revolved fundamentally around pacifism. "We Mennonites don't believe in the use of force."

I stared hard at baby Johann's little gravestone. This was the same man who had demonstrated his belief in the use of force by beating me until I was bloody late into my childhood. And of course, even his assertions about Mennonite pacifism reflected another contradiction. My dad's own brother Herman had served as a pilot in WWII.

Slowly, I pulled myself up off the ground and made my way back to the folks' house. The four of them were sitting around the kitchen table, laughing, with a game called Rummikub set up in front of them.

•••

During those years in the mid-1980s following my divorce from Joe, I became laser focused on two objectives: the well-being of my two children and the success of my academic career.

Shareen had blossomed into a beautiful young woman. She seemed to have no need for the typical rebelliousness of the teenage years. And Stefan, though he missed Joe's help with algebra, seemed happy and well adjusted. One of our favorite things to do together was to wrestle on the floor. He always won.

I commuted from our home in New Jersey to work in the city at NYU, first by train to Hoboken, and then on the Path train to the World Trade Center. My office at the business school was just across the street from the Center. Janice Beyer, a senior colleague in my department and a highly respected member of my profession, lived near us in New Jersey and often rode the train into the city with me.

"You really do need to do something about that wild hair of yours," she said one day as we were sitting on the train next to each other. "You know, I sometimes wonder how you even got a job in such a prestigious business school, looking like that. I've told you this so many times, Marlena. You will never get anywhere as a business school strategy professor if you don't start looking the part. Your kinky, long red hair has got to go. And you need to wear proper business suits, not those totally unsuitable dresses of yours.

You need to look professional, Marlena, or no one will take you seriously."

I looked over at Janice, taking in her prim navy-blue suit, with the little off-white scarf perfectly tied at the neck. Her closed-toe pumps exactly matched the blue of her suit. Her coiffed hair was a flat, uninspired bob, with not a single hair out of place. And her face was made up in an understated, muted way.

To myself, I thought. *You look bland. Boring. Unexciting. No way.* "I know, Jan. I'm sure you're right," I said out loud. She was a senior professor in my department, after all. But I refused to cut my hair or change my wardrobe, just as I had refused to cut my unruly hair back in Asunción when I was eighteen and Pastor Entz told me it presented a sinful temptation for men.

Janice Beyer just shook her head, as I suspect the pastor did those many years ago.

•••

Bill Starbuck, also a senior faculty member at NYU and a leader in the profession, was somehow able to see past my outrageous hair and unconventional clothing.

"You're really good at theory building," he said one day, standing at the open doorway of my office. "You should forget about doing empirical work and stick to generating new theory, like the manuscript from your dissertation that you submitted to the *Administrative Science Quarterly*. How's that going, by the way?"

"Ugh. The editor just asked for a third revision. The more I revise this thing, the less the manuscript reflects anything even resembling a semiotic analysis."

"So what are you going to do about it?" he asked.

"I've been wondering the same thing," I said.

I was facing a dilemma. On one hand, I wanted, even needed, *Administrative Science Quarterly* to publish this manuscript. It, along with an additional article I had already published in another premier journal, would go a long way to ensure a sound base for eventual success in the field, despite my seemingly unprofessional appearance. On the other hand, it had become a watered-down analysis that I was no longer proud of, nor even much interested in.

"Can I show you the letter I'm thinking about sending to the editor?" I handed him the draft letter I had been agonizing over.

Dear Professor Salancik,

You will note that the enclosed manuscript does not follow the reviewers' and your requested changes. In fact, it now more closely resembles my original submission from three rounds back. I have become aware that in the process of attempting to respond to the reviewers' numerous concerns, I departed from semiotic principles to the point where it was no longer an accurate semiotic analysis. It is for this reason that I have reverted closer to what I wrote in my original submission. I trust that my current revisions of the original manuscript help to clarify the methodology, this time without compromising its integrity.

"That's a risky move," he said.

"I feel like I have to take that risk," I said.

In the end, with a few minor additional changes, the editor accepted the manuscript for publication. He told me some time later that he used my case in writing seminars as an illustration of the importance of believing in one's research if it really is sound. And having the courage to stand by it when others call it into question.

•••

Years later, Howard Aldrich and Bill Starbuck, both senior members of the elite group of distinguished scholars elected as Fellows of the Academy of Management (less than 1 percent of the approximately 20,000-member Academy), wrote this in a letter supporting my candidacy to join them as a Fellow:

Marlena Fiol has compiled a distinguished record and demonstrated her exceptional value as a colleague, researcher, and teacher. She is one of the pioneers working at the intersection of cognition and strategy, and she was the first management researcher to make use of semiotic perspectives. She has won national awards for both research and teaching. She has been an intellectual leader in establishing the centrality of cognitive processes in strategy making. Fiol is an innovative and serious researcher who has challenged the field and changed its scholarly direction.

Throughout those years of professional growth, my parents had seemed vaguely pleased to see my apparent success, even though they had little insight into my work. During one of their visits to our home in New Jersey, the three of us were sitting in my backyard, sipping on after-nap cups of coffee together.

"Marlena, this morning I read an article that was lying on your kitchen counter. It was all about the work you're doing on something they were calling *organizational identity*?" Dad's statement turned into a question as he said the last two words. One bushy eyebrow arched as he turned toward me. "It looks like you've done mighty good in your career," he said.

I looked up, surprised. I wasn't engaged in saving souls or saving lives. And yet somehow my parents seemed to understand and appreciate that I had accomplished something of note.

He wasn't finished. "But what Mom and I really appreciate the most is that you aren't uppity and full of pride."

For Mennonites, pride is a sin almost as grave as sexual misconduct. On one hand, I knew all about the sin of arrogance and the exaggerated ego that accompanied it. After all, I had been raised knowing that all good things come from God, rather than our own efforts. On the other, I firmly believed that my own hard work and skills were the source of my success in the still largely male world of business strategy. *Was it possible that these seemingly incompatible perspectives were both true? Could I let go of my own ego enough to allow that maybe, just maybe, I was finally figuring*

out how to use the gifts that God gave me in the first place? That we did
it together?

CHAPTER 15:

Nothing Bad Between Us (1988)

My dad and I

_____

*"The emotion that can break your heart is
sometimes the very one that heals it..."*

—Nicholas Sparks, *At First Sight*

_____

It was a blisteringly hot afternoon in July, one of those days when New Yorkers head out of town en masse to escape the sizzling heat of the city's macadam and concrete. North to the Catskills, over to Rhode Island, or off to the Hamptons.

I heard the whirring of the fan in the corner of my small basement office at NYU, rustling the papers on my desk. My door was partially open, and I could see that some of the hallway lights had been turned off. I glanced at my watch and noticed how late it was. Most of my colleagues had already left for the day.

I picked up the letter and stared again at my father's words in the last paragraph:

> *We're planning a large celebration for our forty-fifth wedding*
> *anniversary at the Alexanderwohl Mennonite Church. Will*

you please be our emcee? We'd like you to highlight the various chapters in our lives, emphasizing how much God has blessed us along the way.

I shuddered and sat back in my chair. I stared at the shelves around me, overflowing with books. Here I was, among my books and papers in my professional world. I was a respected professor of business strategy. How could just those few words shake me to the core and turn me into a humiliated and shamed teenager?

I hadn't stood in front of a Mennonite congregation since that day almost twenty years ago when I had confessed my sinfulness and been banned from participating in church activities. In all these years, no one in my family had ever spoken to me about that shameful moment. And now this invitation to appear again before my father's clan.

I knew it would be a huge affair, as is the Mennonite custom on such occasions. The folks had told me that they'd invited hundreds of people to a *Faspa*, a late afternoon meal of *Zwieback*, sliced ham, cheese, coffee, and *Ploomemos* (cold prune soup), as well as a service in the basement of their church in Goessel, Kansas.

Hundreds of Mennonites, likely including some of the people who had worked with Dad in Paraguay. Who had sat in the congregation on that scorching day in early January of 1970.

I wondered why he hadn't asked my brother David or Mary Lou's husband, both devout Mennonites, to fill this role. Or one of my sisters? Was this his way of offering me a chance to redeem myself? Or was this a test?

"I love you and I wish I could, but I can't do it, Dad," I mumbled to myself as I stood to leave the office.

•••

At home that night, after the kids were in bed, I stared out my kitchen window into the darkness. Finally, I picked up the phone and dialed.

"Hi, Mom. I wanted to talk to you and Dad about me emceeing at your forty-fifth," I said when my mother answered.

"Oh yes, honey, I've been thinking about that, too. Do you think you'll be OK with that? I mean..."

"I think I know what you mean, Mom," I interrupted. "The last time I stood in front of a congregation of Mennonites, it wasn't pretty."

I heard a deep sigh. "Let's not talk about that," she said softly. "Do you want to speak to Dad?"

"Sure. Thanks, Mom," I said, shaking my head. *Let's not talk about that. Even after all these years.*

"Hello, Marlena." My father's brusque voice came over the line.

"Hi, Dad. I was just calling about the emcee thing at your anniversary celebration."

"What about it?" he asked.

"Well..." I paused.

"I want you to do this for us." His voice was low and soft, without its usual clipped sharpness.

In that moment, holding the phone to my ear, I felt the enormity of what was taking place between us. My father not only believed in my abilities, he also trusted that I would honor my mother and him in front of their Mennonite clan.

"I was calling to tell you I couldn't do it, Dad," I whispered. After a pause, I cleared my throat. "But I feel your trust and I appreciate it so much. Can I call you tomorrow to let you know?"

"That'll be fine," he said.

I did want to do this for my father. We had come such a long way, he and I. But that night I couldn't sleep. Every time I closed my eyes, I saw the image of stern, silent people, hundreds of them, seated in dark, squared-off pews, all eyes converging on me, as I sat in front of them on a straight-backed, wooden chair next to the pulpit. Even though a light breeze blew across my bed from an open window, the musty, trapped air of the Paraguayan Mennonite church invaded my senses and I gasped to catch my breath.

"This is crazy," I muttered to myself, sitting up in my bed. "That was then and this is now." I switched on the lamp next to the bed, reached for the tablet of paper and pen that lay next to it and began to write.

All of the reasons why this would be different...

I stared at the blank page. I knew there were lots of reasons. They just weren't coming to me at the moment. But neither was sleep. I finally got up, deciding instead to clean my bathrooms. I never did create that list of all of the ways this would be different. But the next day I found a degree of relief from my misgivings by creating a detailed outline of what I might say.

I called the folks to say that I would do it.

•••

My children and I arrived in Kansas a few days before the celebration. My sister Mary Lou picked us up at the Wichita airport. As we sped north on I-135, I asked as off-handedly as I could, "Did Dad ever say anything to you about why he wanted me to be the emcee for this big event?"

"No. Why do you ask?" If Mary Lou knew anything, she wasn't letting on. So I said nothing in response.

Fortunately, my children in the backseat filled the awkward moment of silence. "Who all is here of our cousins besides your kids, Aunt Mary Lou? When will we see them? How long are they staying?" She responded that my older sister, her husband, and their two children were already here and that one of my brothers with his wife and four children were arriving from Canada later in the day.

Mary Lou honked three times as she turned the car into our parents' driveway. Before she came to a full stop, the front door opened and Mom rushed out onto the porch, wiping her hands on an apron. Right behind her, Dad appeared at the door, a lopsided smile on his face.

At sixteen and twelve, my children still loved visiting their *Grossma* and *Grosspa*. They ran ahead of me to hug them.

"It's so good to see you all," Mom said. "Come in. We have supper all ready for you."

I smiled as I walked up the two rickety steps to their porch and into my parents' embrace. *So much is different*, I thought to myself in that moment. *I'm no longer the broken child who brings shame into their lives. And Dad's no longer the angry man I have to defend myself against.*

●●●

I had just two days to gather some additional firsthand stories to make my program notes come alive. I knew I would find those stories in the boxes of diaries, old letters, and news clippings my parents had stashed in their garage. Dad had parked their car in the driveway to make room for my project.

The door leading into the garage from the kitchen sagged on its hinges and made a squeaking sound when I opened it. Dank mustiness hung in the air. I searched in the semidarkness for a switch and finally pulled a string to light a dim bulb dangling over an uneven workbench. I stood in the middle of the garage and looked around. In one corner I spotted the sawed-off broomstick with a piece of string and a hook tied to the end of it that my folks used to catch small catfish in the pond near their home. Next to it was an assortment of rusty garden implements in neat piles.

Crude mismatched shelves loaded with boxes lined an entire wall. Pushing aside thick spiderwebs, I began to pull them down onto the floor. I sorted through each of them and made several separate piles. Satisfied with what I had found, I sat on the concrete floor of the garage, with the tattered books and papers spread all around me. I sifted through diaries from the early 1940s, when Dad took his new Mennonite bride to the Chaco of Paraguay. I ran across the letter I'd sent them telling them of my divorce from their beloved Steve. Another stack of letters, bound together with a frayed blue string, documented the correspondence between my folks and the Mennonite Central Committee during the time they left their work at Km. 81. At the bottom of one of the boxes was a small photograph of my two children and me, taken the day I married Joe. Someone had carefully cut Joe out of the photo. Just a trace of his red tie still showed behind my left shoulder.

The stifling Kansas summer heat bore down on me like a steamy wet blanket. I was holding my head in my hands when I heard the kitchen door open.

"Mom, what's wrong?" Shareen came in and knelt in front of me, her hands on my shoulders.

"I was just thinking about how many wrong turns I've taken in my life. How much pain I caused others and myself. Like I was blind…"

"I thought you were working on the program for *Grossma* and *Grosspa*," she said, raising her brows questioningly.

"I was. That's what got me thinking about how complicated love is."

"I don't understand," she said.

I looked at my beautiful, almost-grown-up girl. Her long hair was pulled into a thick ponytail at the back of her head. Her full lips were slightly parted, as though wanting to say more, but not knowing what else to say. I knew she was too young to understand the complicated ways that love can manifest in our lives.

"I don't either," I said, smiling through my tears.

Shareen stood up and hugged me. "You OK, Mom?" Her big blue eyes gazed directly into mine.

"Yeah," I said, wiping the remaining tears from my cheeks.

She left the garage and I continued to piece together the threads of my parents' extraordinary lives. Occasionally, my mother came out to bring me an iced coffee or a sandwich. Stefan poked his head through the door once to tell me he was playing basketball at the high school across the street.

Hours later, overheated and exhausted, I tucked all of the boxes back on the rough makeshift shelves and went out for a long walk alone through the deserted streets of the tiny Kansas town. The sun was still fiery despite the late afternoon hour. Jumbled thoughts raced through my mind. "You're such an enigma, Dad," I murmured to myself. "It's obvious you love me very much, probably always have. You special-ordered me, after all. And you hurt me. Damn. You hurt me. And I hurt my kids, whom I love more than my own life. Damn. Love is so complicated."

For a moment, I felt my familiar protective armor coming up and wished I had thought to bring my cigarettes. My shoulders tensed and my steps quickened. And then a question hit me, and I stopped short: *Can I accept that we all hurt those we love? Including me, including Dad?* I took a deep breath and looked around me at the rows of shabby little houses. Feeling my shoulders relax, I turned and slowly made my way back to my folks' house. It occurred to me that maybe it was time to stop numbing myself with nicotine.

That evening, I helped Mom set the little kitchen table for supper. I ladled the *Borscht* she'd made into five melamine bowls she had set out. I heated the *Zwieback* in her rusty, beat-up but functioning toaster oven. Dad and the kids were in the living room, finishing a game of UNO.

"My, that sure smells good," Dad said, putting down his cards and looking up with his lopsided grin.

Is this what it feels like for a heart to run over? I wondered. The warm feeling that spread through me seemed to expand, into the little kitchen and living room, enveloping each of my most beloved ones and holding them there. I wanted the moment never to end.

•••

I had asked my siblings and their families, staying with various relatives in the area, to gather at our parents' house the next day after breakfast to go over the program together. We sat on chairs, boxes, or on the ground in the backyard, passing around the usual gourd of *ter_eré* (the cold version of *yerba mate*) to counter the day's heat already bearing down on us.

"Mom, Dad, you need to leave now. This is all supposed to be a surprise for you," I said, grinning.

"OK. Just don't do anything foolish," Dad said as he moved toward the house. For a moment, I thought he was serious, and a ripple of fear shot through me. But then he turned toward me and I saw his crooked smile.

My brother David and Mary Lou's husband Rusty had both brought their guitars and were quietly strumming the tune of a hymn called "Until Then," which we had chosen has the theme song for the program.

"That sounds great. Here are the lyrics," I said, passing around sheets of paper. Most of us knew it by heart. It was our parents' favorite hymn. We all broke into four-part harmony as though we'd never been apart.

"So, what else do you have planned, Madam Emcee?" *Was there a slight sneer in David's voice or was I imagining it?*

I decided to ignore it. "I thought we could have a skit where eight of the grandchildren play the roles of us kids, and the two oldest, Shareen and John Darwin, play the role of the parents. We can enact how *Grossma* predicted what each of her children would grow up doing: John a farmer, Elisabeth a nurse... You know, down the line..." We all laughed and reminisced about

Mom's predictions and how they had all come true.

"We can work on the skit this afternoon, kids," I said to the children. "Now, here's what I had in mind for the serious part of the program."

Everyone wanted to contribute and, surprisingly to me, no one opposed any of my ideas for the presentations. By noon, we all had our assignments and were satisfied with the result.

"Come have some *Arbüs* and *Rollküake* [watermelon and crullers] for lunch." My mother's voice sounded light and happy.

•••

The morning of the grand celebration, I woke up with a pounding headache. I dragged myself quietly off the sagging pullout couch so as not to awaken Stefan, who was still asleep beside me. Holding my head in my hands, I shuffled to the bathroom and sat on the closed toilet seat. Pressing my palms against the sides of my head, I willed myself to dislodge the traces of last night's nightmare. In the dream, I had a wonderful program all worked out, down to the tiniest details. But when I walked up to the podium to begin welcoming everyone, I saw before me a vast crowd of people wearing black robes and masks, slicing the air with hundreds of angry red spears pointed in my direction.

"*Ach...*" I said out loud, still holding my head in my hands and wishing the present moment, safe in my parents' bathroom, would override the terror of the nightmarish dream.

"Are you OK, Marlena?" It was my mother's voice from the kitchen.

"I'm fine. I'll be out in a minute," I said, fishing through my bag for some Tylenol.

"How's the program coming along?" We were sitting at the breakfast table. Dad seemed casual, unconcerned, just mildly curious.

"It's all put together." My voice sounded more confident than I felt.

"Well, Mother and I, we want you to know how much we appreciate you doing this for us," he said, reaching across the table and placing his hand over mine. *I just hope I don't disappoint you, Dad,* I thought, staring at his hand.

Nothing Bad Between Us

···

For the program, I chose to wear a blue dress that had a collar up close to my neck and that hung appropriately below my knees, exuding quality and professionalism. I let my reddish-brown hair fall around my shoulders and down my back, but I pulled it back from my face enough to reveal the subtle lines of my makeup. *At least I'll look like I'm sure of myself,* I thought, staring into the mirror as I finished applying my lipstick.

At four o'clock, the guests began to arrive. I stood at the front of the church basement on a platform and watched them enter. They looked so familiar, the women with somber dark skirts and the men in dark slacks and button-down shirts. *This could be the same congregation I faced in* Asunción, I thought, *other than the fact that the women are now sitting among the men rather than off to one side.*

I sucked in my breath when I recognized Hans Penner and his wife as they entered the hall. I hadn't heard that they were coming. In fact, I didn't even know that they now lived in Kansas. My face felt flushed. Of all of the Mennonites who worked with my parents in Paraguay, the Penners were probably the most central to every chapter of that work.

And he had been there that day in early January of 1970—next to Heinz Duerksen. He'd been one of my harshest accusers.

"Marlena, I think we're ready to start." My father's voice pulled me back into the present.

I stood tall, took a deep breath, and began. "Thank you so much for being here..."

My folks sat at the front of the room, directly before me. Mom smiled brightly, her eyes shining, as she took in all of the stories and accolades. Dad occasionally put on his crooked half smile, the right side of his mouth sagging.

I felt my professional strength rise as I gradually moved into the role I knew so well in front of a large audience. I played with the people and made them laugh, recalling funny stories, like how our High-German mother never learned to pronounce Low German properly. I reminisced about the hard times during the start-up of Km. 81 and brought them to tears.

I was good and I knew it.

After the program, family members congregated back at my parents' home. The little house was filled with boisterous laughter and numerous conversations in multiple languages going on at the same time. The kitchen table was piled high with leftover food from the celebration.

"*Hasst Du beoobachtet wot...*" "I hadn't seen her in *Joahre...*" "*Wellst Du...quieres algo para comer...*" Low German, English, and Spanish swirled around the house. We often began a sentence in one language and morphed into another language before finishing it. It was just the way my family interacted, because some of our in-laws spoke only German, some only Spanish, and others only English.

David walked toward me from across the room. "You did a great job emceeing, Marlena," he said, placing an arm around my shoulders.

"Thanks, David. That means a lot to me," I said, kissing him lightly on the cheek.

In the midst of all of the havoc, Dad seemed slightly bewildered, sitting off by himself at the end of the sofa. I caught him looking at me and left the conversation with David to sit next to him.

We sat side-by-side on their worn, dusty-pink sofa with squeaky springs that sagged in the middle. Just sat there, silent, watching the commotion around us. I grabbed his hand, a hand with the big knuckles and thick veins running across it, like lots of crisscrossing dark blue rivers.

"*Doa ess nuscht tsweschen ons,* [There is nothing bad between us,]" I said hoarsely in our native *Plautdietsch.*

"*Ne, doa ess nuscht tweschen ons,*" Dad repeated.

After that, we always spoke those words to each other at every goodbye.

Nothing Bad Between Us

EPILOGUE (2001–2003)

Our family in 2001 on the veranda of our Km. 81 house

"We shall not cease from exploration, and the end
of all our exploring will be to arrive where we
started and know the place for the first time."

—T. S. Eliot, *Four Quartets*

When my dad turned ninety in 2001, the leprosy station and I both turned fifty. There was to be a grand celebration at Km. 81 to mark this milestone of the leprosy work. Naturally, Mom and Dad flew to Paraguay to be there. All eight of us children were there as well.

For me, this big event was not so much about celebrating the leprosy work. Rather, it represented a homecoming. It was an occasion for me to reflect on the dark and lonely chapter that had been the first thirty years of my life, punctuated by interludes of safety in my forest-home as a child and in the decade-long routine hum of my first marriage. To arrive where I started, as T.S. Eliot said, and know the place for the first time.

My brother Wesley met me at the airport. He was an important doctor in Paraguay now, even advising the country's president on medical issues. I watched his straight back and brisk gait as he walked ahead of me to his car in the airport parking lot. I smiled. It was just like our dad used to walk.

We made our way the eighty-one kilometers east of Asunción to the leprosy station. I hadn't been to the station in many years. Along the highway, nothing seemed changed. The *Ruta* was still narrow and rough with deep potholes. My brother leaned almost incessantly on his car horn as we wove around cars, buses, motorcycles and ox-drawn carts.

We turned left at the Km. 81 marker onto the familiar narrow dirt road. A few buildings, low brick structures with tin roofs, stood near the *Ruta*. The dirt road curved its way up a gently sloping hill, deep ruts making it a road easier to maneuver on foot than by car. My mind wandered to the many times a bus from Asunción had dropped me off at the Km. 81 marker and I had walked the two and a half kilometers up this road from the *Ruta* to the station.

All around was a mostly barren landscape with wild grass and little clumps of scrappy trees, not the rain forest trees found farther east in Brazil, but also not the dry brush of the Chaco of west Paraguay. We passed over a small bridge that crossed what used to be the stream we swam in as kids. It had long since dried up. The boards were loose. We clattered across it and made our way up a steep hill. Abruptly, on our left as far as we could see were rows of blossoming orange trees and mulberry bushes exploding with purple bounty. On our right were fields of corn, the stalks just beginning to push their way through the rich red soil.

At the top of the hill, we drove through a thick grove of mango trees; then, in front of us lay what looked like a quaint little German village with neatly trimmed hedges and raked dirt walkways around each of the homes. Nearby barns were filled with fine breeds of horses and cattle. Large garden plots displayed precise rows of carrots, green beans, onions and *mandioca*, a root vegetable that was a daily staple in our diet when I was a kid. Everything looked much tidier and fancier than I remembered it.

•••

The celebration at the leprosy station was a huge affair, with friends, colleagues, and government officials in attendance from all over Paraguay and other parts of the world. Preparations for it clearly had been going on for a very long time. Km. 81 looked like a resort, with freshly whitewashed buildings, manicured lawns and bushes, and bright-colored flowers. Brazilian *Portulaca*, with its tube-like leaves, sent large flamboyant flowers shooting from the ends of sprawling stems. *Pentas*, called starflowers in the US, showed off their hairy foliage and bunches of star-shaped flowers in bright tones of lavender, red, white, and pink. Cockscombs were blooming everywhere; the softly textured bushes were bursting with flowers in shades of purple, yellow, orange, and pink. It was a veritable feast for the eyes.

Dad had suffered a slight stroke some weeks before the event, right after he and Mom had arrived in Paraguay. So by the time the rest of us got there, he was disoriented and had a hard time communicating. Although he seemed to understand the purpose of the event, he appeared uninterested in it. He knew who each one of his children was, but remained mostly off to the side, alone, a blank look on his face.

We were headed for the large auditorium that the station workers had prepared for the occasion. "I can't believe what they have done to this place," Dad muttered as he stumbled along beside me through the profusion, holding onto my arm for support.

Thinking he was pleased to see how beautiful the grounds were, I said, "Yes, it's pretty, isn't it?"

"*Ne! Dot ess veschwenderisch,*" he said, mouthing the words emphatically, even if with some difficulty. He would always revert to *Plautdietsch* when he was angry, as do I. I've always thought it was a much more expressive language for anger than English. "It's a waste. That's not being good stewards of the money people contribute for this mission work. That cannot be God's will."

I pressed his arm close. At that moment, I was filled with love and compassion for this dear man by my side, my father, who even in his impaired physical and mental condition, stuck to his strong Christian convictions and wasn't afraid to say so.

At the same time, I was aware that his words were tinged with resentment. Did my father resent that this place, *his* leprosy station, scarcely resembled what he had built? He had practically single-handedly planted the trees, planned the construction of the buildings, and organized the grounds fifty years ago. The trees were still here; the buildings still stood. But the place looked nothing like it had when we lived here.

For the hundreds of people who came for the grand event, this was an occasion to commemorate the work that my parents had pioneered fifty years ago. Various prominent officials gave speeches. Then it was time for our father to address the crowd. My oldest brother John stood and turned toward Dad to offer his arm for support. Dad clung to John's arm as a small child might who is just learning to walk. Everyone watched in silence as, very slowly, they made their way together onto the stage. The stillness in the auditorium was palpable.

"Our father welcomes you and thanks you for being here." I could tell that my brother was making it up. "He wishes he could speak to you, but it is difficult for him at this time." Dad just looked bewildered.

When my mother joined them on the stage, she gave a cheery speech about how important this work had been to them. Then she called each of us, her eight children, to stand so she could introduce us. *As though we had anything to do with the leprosy work.*

I stared down at my lap. My eyes locked onto the narrow gold band on the finger of my left hand. I had met my husband and soulmate ten years before, and although he wasn't able to be there, I felt his presence. "I am so grateful," I murmured under my breath. "So grateful for who I am and for what I have today."

"And this is Marlena." My mother was smiling, gesturing for me to stand and turn to face the audience. "She lives in Denver, Colorado, with her husband Ed."

I pushed myself up off my chair, keeping my eyes on the floor.

Mom asked each of us to remain standing until she had introduced all of us. When she finished the introductions, the eight of us broke into applause for our parents. I raised my eyes at that point and briefly scanned the rows and rows of people staring at us. And then I saw him: Hans Thiessen, the man with whom I'd committed the sins that got me into trouble with the Mennonite church over three decades ago, was sitting a third of the way back on the left side, staring straight at me. His hair had thinned, and his cheeks looked hollow. As I met the gaze of the first man I ever thought I loved, the man who betrayed me and left me with nothing but a venereal disease, I felt nothing. No disgust. No hatred. Not even antipathy. It was as though the person standing here staring at him were altogether someone other than the young girl who had once thought she knew him.

After the formal program ended, huge piles of food were served to the masses. It was a traditional Paraguayan feast: Boiled *mandioca* (a potato-like root), *asado de carne* (barbecued meat), cabbage slaw, and *sopa paraguaya* (a cheesy cornbread). People wandered around the grounds as they ate.

I made my way alone past what used to be the forest where I had constructed my own little safe haven as a kid. The trees were gone; they had been completely cleared. At the end of the path, however, the familiar red brick L-shaped house that used to be our home looked unchanged. No one was there, so I walked around to the veranda side of the house. I sat on the concrete steps and allowed my thoughts to wander.

I stared at the wooden door to what had once been the girls' bedroom at the end of the veranda. Instinctively, I pulled my arms around my chest, as though protecting the small child who used to sleep in that room. My eyes moved over to my parents' bedroom next door. I thought about the many occasions when we kids made too much noise during siesta time and Dad stormed out of that room, shouting for us to be quiet. I remembered the strap that hung on a hook in the back of their bedroom, near the washbasin. An involuntary shudder rippled through my body. I looked over at the hedge, still the same, where I had vomited after almost every meal during those painful weeks before my twin was removed from my body. And I stared at the spot on the veranda where my parents and I stood the afternoon that Dad kicked me out of his life, telling me there were plenty of other children for him to love.

A tear and then another made their ways slowly down my cheeks. I felt none of the old familiar shame about being sinful, nor did I feel anger about having been mistreated. In that moment, I was filled with deep tenderness and compassion for the young child who never seemed to be able to find her place here and for her father, who didn't know how to manage his rebellious daughter.

The sound of approaching laughter and boisterous yelling interrupted my reverie. I wanted more time alone on that veranda, to feel the salve of compassionate memory. But soon the rest of my family was there, and the ten of us posed for a happy-family photo on the steps of the veranda.

After another set of programs and more food, the crowd began to break up. I found Dad sitting alone on a bench off to the side, wiping drool from his mouth. I sat down next to him. Although he still sat with his back as erect as always, he leaned slightly in toward me. We said nothing, just sat there quietly.

I knew it was time for me to let him go. Mingled with the sadness of that moment was a profound sense of gratitude. I inhaled deeply and reached for his hand.

•••

My parents stayed in Paraguay after the Km. 81 celebration because my father became too weak to travel back to the States. May of 2003 was the last time I visited them there before my dad died.

He still read the newspapers. He still seemed interested in what was happening around the world. But he was a shadow of the man he once had been. His body had always been slender, but strong; now it was frail. His dark eyes had almost entirely lost their penetrating sharpness. We spoke hardly at all. He showed little overt affection but seemed comfortable with me sitting beside him for hours. Sometimes he rested his arm on my shoulders.

Even now, my parents were engaged in service to others. Each day they both took their walkers over to the old people's home nearby. Mom read to the old folks, and together they sang hymns for them. Many of those old folks were considerably younger than my parents. I'm not sure Mom and Dad ever thought about that.

The last time I went along to sing with them, we all sat on wooden benches in a circle, about twenty of us. A half dozen or so were in wheelchairs. The people in that circle were all elderly German Mennonites, many of whom had been young when my dad first landed in the Chaco of west Paraguay to be their doctor.

Some of them had spent some time doing voluntary service at the leprosy station in east Paraguay and had known me as a young child. Occasionally,

Nothing Bad Between Us

they would remember something about me and, all excited, would call me over to tell me about it. Tina, one of the women who had cared for me when I was little, said to me that last time I sat in their circle, "You always had such sparkly dark eyes. You still do."

I hadn't thought of myself as a Mennonite since the blistering summer day in 1970 when my church in Asunción banned that eighteen-year-old girl from singing in the choir and from playing the organ. But here I was, in a circle of singing Mennonites, feeling oddly at home.

I loved those hymn-singing times. Dad seemed to come to life when he sang. He would throw his head back, close his eyes, and sing the hymns from memory. I sat next to him so that I could feel the vibrations of his still-resonant tenor voice. I melded my voice with his until it felt like we were one. *Nothing between us.* If he launched into the soprano part, which he often did if no one in the circle was leading with a strong voice, I would sing tenor. If he chose the tenor role, I would sing soprano or alto. In and out. Effortlessly. I felt like we were floating together.

In that moment, as I reflected on how completely we had come together, my father and I, I was aware that at some level we had never been disconnected. The brutal intensity of the anger and defiance that characterized our relationship during my youth could never have existed had we not been deeply connected to one another.

I blinked hard a few times and looked over at him sitting next to me. *I know this man so well*, I thought to myself, *because I am so very much like him.* Underneath all of my defiance, there had always been a fierce longing to love and to be loved by this man. But I also knew that he and I had both needed to have our protective armor beaten down by hard knocks in life before we finally were able to acknowledge our own internal demons and become vulnerable with one another.

I smiled and turned back to my songbook.

•••

It was time to say goodbye. My oldest brother John was to take me to the bus stop. My parents and I had already hugged goodbye. They stood side by side in front of a brushy hedge as I stepped up into my brother's dusty old pickup, both of them gripping their walkers. Mom was bent over, while Dad's back was as straight as it had ever been. He wore an old blue stretched-out Kansas wheat farmer cap. The mid-day Chaco sun beat down on them, bathing them in blinding brightness and suffocating heat. Mom's lips quivered ever so slightly. I couldn't tell if there were tears since they both wore flip-down dark glasses.

Tears running down my cheeks, I rolled down the window, turned to Dad and said, "*Doa ess nuscht...*"

Before I could finish, Dad stumbled forward against his walker, grasped it even more firmly with both hands to keep from falling, and roughly whispered, "*Doa ess nuscht tweschen ons.*"

"There's nothing bad between us."

P.S.

Leprosy is a disease that begins as an invisible, imperceptible infection. It affects the nerves of the hands, feet, and eyes, as well as some of the nerves in the skin. In severe, untreated cases, loss of sensation, muscle paralysis of hands and feet, disfigurement, and blindness occur. Eventually the untreated disease dominates patients' lives, leaving them crippled, grossly deformed, and socially rejected.

In the Bible, the word leprosy is mentioned more than forty times. Ancient Israelites believed God inflicted the curse of leprosy on people for the sins they committed. Lepers were rejected and treated as outcasts. This persisted and was still the dominant practice when my folks began their leprosy work in Paraguay in 1951.

Whether or not one believes the biblical accounts of leprosy to be literally true, they provide a metaphor for patterns of sin and separation in and around my own life. In this book, I described a wound festering within me as a young child, the most rebellious of my father's eight children. It erupted into unacceptable behaviors, including adulterous sins as a young girl. The result was rejection, but not only the predictable rejection from my strict father and his Mennonite clan. I rejected myself just as surely as I had witnessed our leprosy patients renouncing themselves in their flawed states.

Biblical accounts of leprosy fortunately also provide a metaphor for the healing power of humility and gratitude. In the seventeenth chapter of the Bible's book of Luke, ten lepers called out in their utter brokenness, "Master, have mercy on us." They were cleansed of their disease. But Luke tells us that only one of the ten returned to offer thanks, thereby attaining not only a lack of disease, but also wellness ("Your faith has made you well"). Similarly, my own brokenness and my father's gradual weakening, which opened us both up to greater humility and gratitude, were important stepping-stones in our journey toward cleansing and wellness.

One of my sisters has told me that she strongly disapproves of me "dredging up for public consumption" the various failures I have described in the book. That has always been the way of our family: Never talk about the bad stuff, the complicated stuff. Put a wall around it to avoid the pain and to appear to live up to our revered Mennonite and broader societal ideals. As painful as parts of this story may be, especially for people devoted to my father and his Mennonite church, I believe as my spiritual teacher, Fr. Richard Rohr, said in a recent meditation, "Wisdom is where you see it *all* and you eliminate none of it and include all of it as important training. Finally, everything belongs. You are able to say, from some larger place that surprises even you, it is what it is, and even the bad was good."

ACKNOWLEDGEMENTS

My grateful acknowledgements go first and foremost to my husband and soulmate, who never doubted that I could do this. Ed, thank you for believing in me, for your encouragement along the way, and for your relentless critique of every word in this book. I couldn't have done any of it without you.

I was blessed with smart and patient readers of my early drafts. Thank you, Linda Atwell, Terri Griffith, and Rita Berglund for not laughing at early versions of my lumpy prose.

Heartfelt thanks to my teachers, Melissa Hart, Jeniffer Thompson, Marni Freedman, Lisa Ohlen Harris, and Tom Jenks. And to my agent, Robert Mackwood, for finding Mango Publishing.

James Scheibli and Dan Blank, I never knew what book marketing meant until I met you. Thank you for helping me find readers interested in my story.

And finally, my thanks go to Brenda Knight at Mango Publishing, for the kick in the butt I needed to get this thing off the ground.

ABOUT THE AUTHOR

Marlena Fiol, PhD, is the author of the inspiring memoir *Nothing Bad Between Us*. Her book is a narrative exploration of her own identity journey from a tortured and rebellious childhood as a Mennonite missionary kid on a leprosy compound in Paraguay, to eventual reconciliation with her people and within herself.

Marlena has written dozens of articles exploring the themes of loss, suffering, healing, learning, love, redemption, and reconciliation. Before becoming a writer of literary essays and blogs, she received worldwide acclaim for her work on learning and identity. This work examined how people within and around organizations make sense of who they are in relation to others, and how that sense of self can change.

Marlena and her husband Ed find both light playfulness and intense joy in their relationships with their grandchildren. They currently spend summers in lush, green Oregon and winters in sunny Arizona. You can learn more about Marlena and her work at marlenafiol.com.

Mango Publishing, established in 2014, publishes an eclectic list of books by diverse authors—both new and established voices—on topics ranging from business, personal growth, women's empowerment, LGBTQ studies, health, and spirituality to history, popular culture, time management, decluttering, lifestyle, mental wellness, aging, and sustainable living. We were recently named 2019 *and* 2020's #1 fastest growing independent publisher by *Publishers Weekly*. Our success is driven by our main goal, which is to publish high quality books that will entertain readers as well as make a positive difference in their lives.

Our readers are our most important resource; we value your input, suggestions, and ideas. We'd love to hear from you—after all, we are publishing books for you!

Please stay in touch with us and follow us at:

Facebook: Mango Publishing
Twitter: @MangoPublishing
Instagram: @MangoPublishing
LinkedIn: Mango Publishing
Pinterest: Mango Publishing

Newsletter: mangopublishinggroup.com/newsletter

Join us on Mango's journey to reinvent publishing, one book at a time.

CPSIA information can be obtained
at www.ICGtesting.com
Printed in the USA
BVHW080414071020
590415BV00002B/2

9 781642 503586